BRIDGES
AND
TUNNELS

INVESTIGATE FEATS OF ENGINEERING

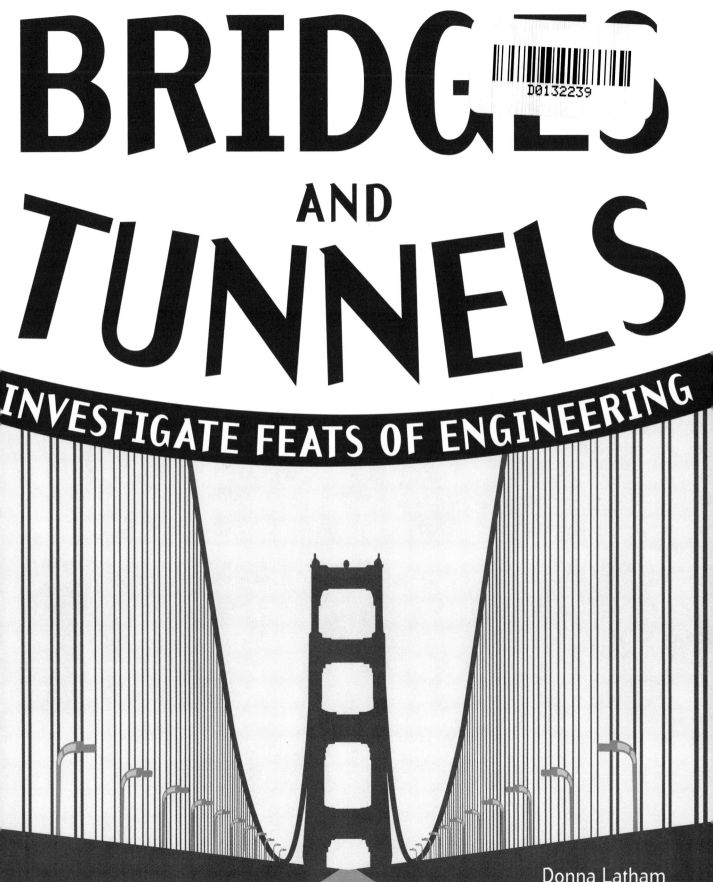

Donna Latham
Illustrated by Jen Vaughn

~ Titles in the *Build It Yourself* Series ~

green press
INITIATIVE

Nomad Press is committed to preserving ancient forests and natural resources. We elected to print *Bridges and Tunnels: Investigate Feats of Engineering* on Thor PCW containing 30% post consumer waste.

Nomad Press made this paper choice because our printer, Sheridan Books, is a member of Green Press Initiative, a nonprofit program dedicated to supporting authors, publishers, and suppliers in their efforts to reduce their use of fiber obtained from endangered forests.

For more information, visit **www.greenpressinitiative.org**.

This book was manufactured by Sheridan Books,
Ann Arbor, MI USA.
April 2013, Job #347425
ISBN: 978-1-936749-51-5

Illustrations by Jen Vaughn
Educational Consultant, Marla Conn

Questions regarding the ordering of this book should be addressed to
Independent Publishers Group
814 N. Franklin St.
Chicago, IL 60610
www.ipgbook.com

Nomad Press
2456 Christian St.
White River Junction, VT 05001
www.nomadpress.net

CONTENTS

Sincere thanks to environmental scientist, cheerleader extraordinaire, and first reader Nick Longo and to physicist Eric Prebys, Ph.D, at Fermilab in Batavia, Illinois.

HAVE YOU EVER DRIVEN ACROSS
a long **bridge** and wondered, "How did they build this?" Have you ever felt excited when driving through a dark **tunnel**? Bridges and tunnels are marvels of design and tributes to human **ingenuity**. Some are so impressive that they are the first thing people think of when they hear the name of a city. Once you see the Golden Gate Bridge in San Francisco, you never forget it!

WORDS to KNOW

bridge: a structure built to span natural or manmade obstacles such as rivers, bays, canyons, highways, and railways.

tunnel: a passageway that goes through or under natural or manmade obstacles such as rivers, mountains, roads, and buildings.

ingenuity: being clever, original, and inventive.

Across the globe, school buses loaded with kids and motorists on their way to jobs depend on bridges and tunnels to get where they need to go. Every day, people walk across bridges or peddle over them on bikes. Trains filled with **commuters** zoom through tunnels that connect sprawling suburbs with bustling cities.

Bridges and tunnels are lifelines that connect people and places.

WORDS to KNOW

commuter: a person who regularly travels from one place to another to get to and from work.

BCE: put after a date, BCE stands for Before Common Era and counts down to zero. CE stands for Common Era and counts up from zero. The year this book is published is 2012 CE.

architect: someone who designs large structures and provides advice on construction.

Some tunnels even deliver water supplies over long distances. As long ago as 520 **BCE**, the ancient Greek **architect** Eupalinos of Megara confronted a staggering challenge. He needed a way to deliver water from its source at a far-away spring to Samos, an ancient city that today is called Pythagorion. But an obstacle loomed: how could he get the clay pipes that would carry the freshwater through the towering mountain that stood in the way?

His problem sparked an idea. He became the first **engineer** to design a plan for digging a tunnel from opposite ends. No one knows exactly how Eupalinos did it because no written records survive. Some experts believe Eupalinos drove wooden boards into the ground and may have placed an early kind of **level** on top of them to determine the horizontal **plane**. Eupalinos might also have used the ancient Greek surveying instrument called a dioptra. The dioptra contained **protractors** that measured angles in vertical and horizontal planes.

Whatever his method, Eupalinos' plan proved incredibly precise.

WORDS to KNOW

engineer: someone who uses science and math to design and construct structures such as buildings, bridges, and tunnels.

level: a tool made with a tube that holds liquid with an air bubble. It is used to measure a horizontal plane.

plane: a flat or level surface.

protractor: a semicircular instrument used to measure and construct angles.

surveyor: someone who uses math to measure angles, distances, and elevations on the earth's surfaces.

geometry: the branch of math that looks at the relationship of points, lines, surfaces, and shapes.

DID YOU KNOW?

Long before he became the first President of the United States, George Washington worked as a **surveyor**. As a boy, he studied **geometry** and surveying. In 1768, when he was 16 years old, Washington began surveying land in Virginia.

WORDS to KNOW

World Heritage Site: a place listed by the United Nations Educational, Scientific and Cultural Organization (UNESCO) as having special cultural or physical importance.

arch: a curved structure in the shape of an upside-down U.

structure: a bridge, tunnel, building, or other object built from a number of different parts that are put together in a certain way.

engineering: the work an engineer does, using science and math to design and construct structures.

innovation: a new product or way of doing something.

natural resource: something from nature that people can use in some way, such as water, stone, and wood.

manmade: something made by humans, such as plastic and glass.

force: a push or pull that changes an object's motion.

Two groups of workers using axes and chisels met almost exactly at the center. After adjusting the height of the tunnels just a bit, the two ends were connected. Today, the Tunnel of Eupalinos is a **World Heritage Site** and a popular tourist destination.

A few hundred years later, engineers in the Roman Empire (27 BCE–393 CE) constructed magnificent **arch** bridges. Their armies relied on these bridges to conquer new lands. Many of these **structures** survive to this day.

ENGINEERING

Engineering is both science and art. Early engineers and architects were masters of **innovation**. They rose to monumental challenges by dreaming big. They thought of ideas no one had thought of before. Building massive structures like bridges and tunnels was one way early engineers figured out ingenious ways to overcome barriers. Using **natural resources**, **manmade** materials, and the **forces** of nature, engineers have come up with ways to keep tunnels from caving in and bridges from falling down.

WORDS to KNOW

technology: scientific or mechanical tools and methods used to do something.

trial-and-error: trying first one thing, then another and another, until something works.

evolve: to change or develop slowly, over time.

physics: the science of how matter and energy work together. Matter is what an object is made of. Energy is the ability to perform work.

modification: a change.

Engineers constantly improve **technology** by building on earlier discoveries. They depend on **trial-and-error**. They collect and share knowledge from past successes and failures in design, building materials, machines, and tools. Building materials, for example, are constantly **evolving**. Early people depended on branches, rocks, and other materials found in nature to build bridges. Later, when steel was invented, it became the material of choice for many bridges. In this way technological advances have continued through the centuries.

Over time, engineers began to apply their knowledge of **physics** to their designs. Even so, many bridges and tunnels have collapsed during hurricanes, earthquakes, and floods. Engineers are always working to make lifesaving **modifications** to design structures so that they can better withstand the forces of nature.

Notable Quotable

"Creativity is thinking up new things. Innovation is doing new things."
—*Business professor and management expert Harold J. Leavitt*

EPIC STRUGGLES

In the past, building gigantic structures required **Herculean** efforts. Courageous builders worked at mind-boggling heights above rolling waters. They dug deep into the earth. Many placed their lives at risk over and over again. Some did not survive falls or explosions. Others, such as the engineer of the famous Brooklyn Bridge in New York, were tragically injured. But all left an incredible **legacy** that lasts today.

WORDS to KNOW

Herculean: great strength or effort.

legacy: something handed down that has long-lasting impact.

Use the activities in this book to make your own discoveries about marvels of engineering. Along the way you'll learn about the engineering process. Let your ideas spark your own innovations. Most of the projects in this book involve items that you might have around the house. Remember that safety's first, so ask adults for help when handling pins, nails, screwdrivers, and other sharp objects.

ENGINEERING AND THINKING BIG

YOU PROBABLY DON'T REALIZE HOW FASCINATING THE engineering profession really is. Engineers use science and math, but they also use experience, judgment, and common sense to make things that are useful and that benefit people.

Notable Quotable

"Scientists study the world as it is; engineers create the world that has never been."
—*Theodore van Kármán, physicist and aerospace engineer*
who made major contributions to the United States Space Program

Engineers come up with creative and practical solutions to technical problems. They design and build structures, machines, and systems. They create amazing products and ensure that these products are safe. Engineers develop things we depend on and use all the time, such as cozy dog beds filled with stuffing made from recycled soda pop bottles. Or surgical tweezers that allow doctors to make precise incisions in the human eye. Using properties of light, engineers build lasers. By applying principles of **chemistry**, they improve medicines.

BRANCHES OF ENGINEERING

According to the U.S. Department of Labor, Bureau of Statistics, engineers hold about 1.6 million jobs in the United States. The field of engineering is constantly changing, but it includes five major branches: chemical, civil, computer, electrical, and mechanical.

DID YOU KNOW?

Nearly everything we use and depend on has been engineered. This includes things like roller coasters, smart phones, running shoes, and even methods of keeping food safe. But engineering is called "the stealth profession." That's because engineers work behind the scenes. We hardly ever hear about the talented but "invisible" engineers who devise many of the creations on which we all rely.

BRANCHES OF ENGINEERING

CHEMICAL	Using science to convert **raw materials** and chemicals into things people can use, such as food and energy products.
CIVIL	Designing and building bridges, buildings, dams, highways, and tunnels.
COMPUTER	Designing technology, such as computer software and hardware, operating systems, and computer networks.
ELECTRICAL	Designing electrical systems and electronic products.
MECHANICAL	Designing mechanical systems, such as engines, tools, and machines.

THE ENGINEERING DESIGN PROCESS

Engineering is a group effort. It allows for the open exchange of ideas. The Engineering Design Process is a series of steps engineers follow when they tackle a problem. The steps lead to a **solution**, which is often a new product, system, or structure. Specific steps might vary, but they typically involve identifying a problem, brainstorming, designing, building a **prototype**, testing, evaluating, and redesigning.

WORDS to KNOW

solution: an answer to a problem.

prototype: a working model or mock-up that allows engineers to test their solution.

open-ended: able to adapt to the needs of a situation.

- ° **IDENTIFY THE PROBLEM:** In the first step, engineers figure out what they need to accomplish. They pose questions to target their goal. They engage in fact-finding by conducting research and collecting information.

- ° **BRAINSTORM POSSIBLE SOLUTIONS:** Now, engineers let their ideas fly like lightning. In a group, they share creative and sudden ideas, no matter how "impossible" they may seem. One clever idea can spark unexpected solutions or methods. After brainstorming, engineers sort through the ideas to target the most likely solution and focus on it.

- ° **DESIGN AND DRAW A PLAN:** At this step, engineers draw a diagram of the solution to their problem. They note which tools and building materials are required to proceed.

- **BUILD A PROTOTYPE:** A prototype is an important component of testing and research. It allows engineers to notice a missing piece they might have overlooked. Others can share their ideas for improvement or see something that might not work.

- **TEST THE PROTOTYPE:** As a team, engineers conduct tests. They observe how the prototype measures up to the design.

- **EVALUATE THE OUTCOME:** At this step, engineers discuss what worked or didn't work with the design. They share ideas for improvements in design and materials.

- **REDESIGN WITH IMPROVEMENTS:** Engineers apply ideas for improvement and develop a stronger product to test.

ENGINEERING DESIGN PROCESS

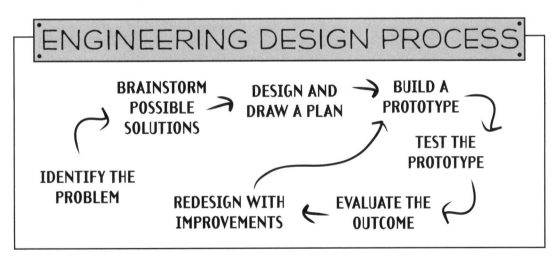

Do you notice how the Engineering Design Process flow chart connects the steps with arrows? That keeps the design process **open-ended**. Engineers might have to throw out one idea and come up with a new solution. They might double back to revisit a step or two. An earlier idea that was rejected might turn out to be promising. Frequently, several solutions are possible, so engineers devise multiple solutions.

CIVIL ENGINEERING

Civil engineering is called the "mother of all engineering disciplines." It's considered the oldest branch, which gave birth to all the others. Civil engineers design, construct, and maintain bridges, buildings, dams, highways, and tunnels. Civil engineers confront problems by asking questions such as: How can we build a passage when there's a sprawling canyon in the way? How can we build an underwater tunnel that won't cave in? How can we design a bridge that will withstand an earthquake?

FORCES: PUSHES AND PULLS

Physics is a branch of science that deals with the physical world. It centers on **matter** and **energy** and their **interactions**. Engineers apply the principals of physics to build structures that resist forces. A force is a push or pull. Forces, which make things move or change position, are exerted on big structures like bridges and tunnels. These forces are called **loads**.

If structures aren't able to withstand the load, they will split apart and fall down.

WORDS to KNOW

matter: a substance that takes up space.

energy: the ability to do work.

interaction: how things work together.

load: an applied force or weight.

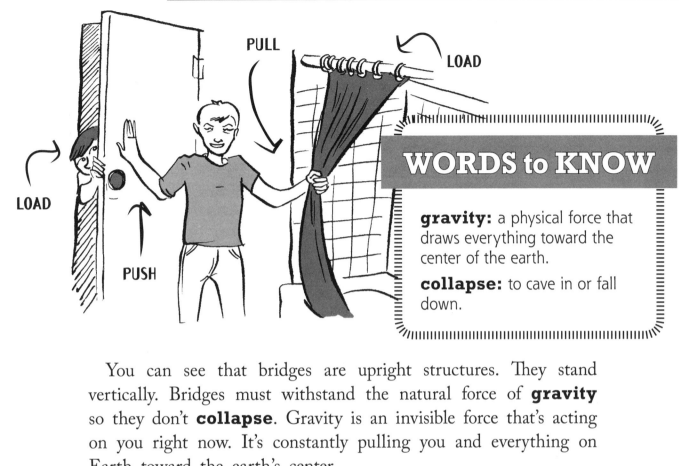

PULL

LOAD

LOAD

PUSH

WORDS to KNOW

gravity: a physical force that draws everything toward the center of the earth.

collapse: to cave in or fall down.

You can see that bridges are upright structures. They stand vertically. Bridges must withstand the natural force of **gravity** so they don't **collapse**. Gravity is an invisible force that's acting on you right now. It's constantly pulling you and everything on Earth toward the earth's center.

Bridges also have to remain upright in ferocious weather. They must endure winds that twist them. And they must battle natural disasters, including earthquakes, that violently push them from side to side. Underground, tunnels must resist caving in.

Collapse is a reality for both bridges and tunnels.

TENSION AND COMPRESSION

WORDS to KNOW

tension: a pulling force that pulls or stretches a material outward.

compression: a pushing force that squeezes or presses a material inward.

Tension and **compression** are the primary forces that keep structures standing—and that cause them to fall down. Tension is a pulling force. It pulls a material outward. When you pull on a piece of string or a stretchy rubber band, you'll see that it grows longer under the tension. Tension stretches material apart—so much that it usually grows longer and can even break or snap.

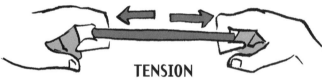

TENSION

Snapping occurs when the force of tension overcomes an object's ability to handle the stretching. When you twist and stretch that piece of string or rubber band with too much force, it will split apart and snap.

Compression is a pushing force. It pushes a material inward, squeezing it together and usually causing it to become shorter. When you squash an empty beverage can, you're using compression. When vehicles and pedestrians travel over bridges, they create both tension and compression. Supporting the weight of their own roadways causes tension and compression on bridges, too.

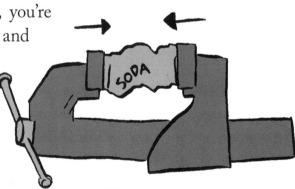

COMPRESSION

When the force of compression overcomes an object's capacity to handle the pressure, buckling occurs. This is when an object starts to crumble. You can push on a soda can a certain amount and it can take it. But push harder, and at some point it can't take the pressure and the can buckles.

If building materials begin to break down and buckle, a structure is in danger of collapse. When a blizzard dumps 18 inches of heavy snow on a house (46 centimeters), the roof might buckle and cave in under the pressure.

TRY THIS

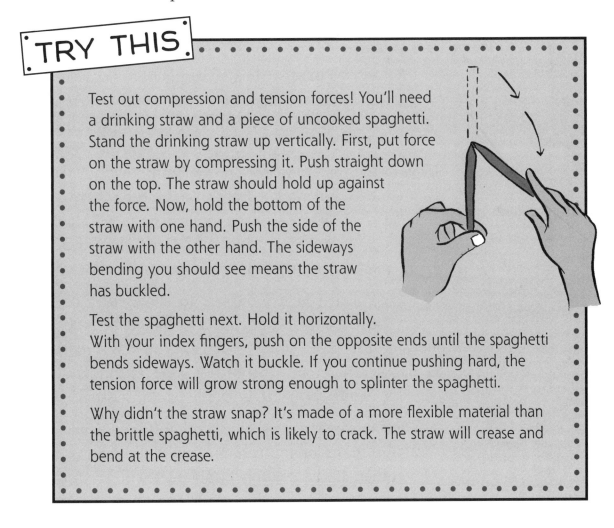

Test out compression and tension forces! You'll need a drinking straw and a piece of uncooked spaghetti. Stand the drinking straw up vertically. First, put force on the straw by compressing it. Push straight down on the top. The straw should hold up against the force. Now, hold the bottom of the straw with one hand. Push the side of the straw with the other hand. The sideways bending you should see means the straw has buckled.

Test the spaghetti next. Hold it horizontally. With your index fingers, push on the opposite ends until the spaghetti bends sideways. Watch it buckle. If you continue pushing hard, the tension force will grow strong enough to splinter the spaghetti.

Why didn't the straw snap? It's made of a more flexible material than the brittle spaghetti, which is likely to crack. The straw will crease and bend at the crease.

• DID YOU KNOW?

Concrete is a building material that can take a lot of compression. But because it can become brittle and crack, it cannot handle a lot of tension. Steel bars called rebar are added to concrete to make it stronger. This reinforced concrete doesn't crack and break apart as easily as regular concrete under the forces of tension and **shear**. There is one drawback of rebar, though. It makes old concrete difficult to recycle when it's no longer useful.

WORDS to KNOW

shear: a sliding force that slips parts of a material in opposite directions.

torsion: a twisting force that turns or twirls a material.

TORSION AND SHEAR

Torsion is a twisting force. When you wring out a wet towel, you're applying torsion. When strong winds cause torsion, bridges are in danger of twisting so violently that they fall down. Shear is a sliding force. When shear is applied to an object, parts of it slide past each other and there is force going in different directions.

TORSION

SHEAR

When you use scissors to cut a sheet of paper, you're using shear force. The handles of the scissors move in opposite directions. They place force on the screw that joins the handles together. The blades slide to cut the paper. The word shears is a synonym for scissors.

When an earthquake shakes a column supporting a building, parts of the column might slip against one another. If the column tumbles, it will be the first step to the building's disastrous collapse.

EARTHQUAKE ENGINEERING

Earthquake engineering is a subcategory of civil engineering. Earthquake engineers apply engineering principles to build structures and systems that withstand earthquakes. They design and construct airports, buildings, bridges, water systems, and more.

To help engineers learn more about the effects of earthquakes on structures, scientists in Miki City, Japan, think big. And they build big. They developed the world's largest shake table, called the E-Defense. Shake tables test the effects of earthquakes on structures. They help scientists understand the abilities of different structures to resist **seismic** shaking, which occurs during an earthquake.

WORDS to KNOW

seismic: caused by Earth's vibrations and tremors during an earthquake.

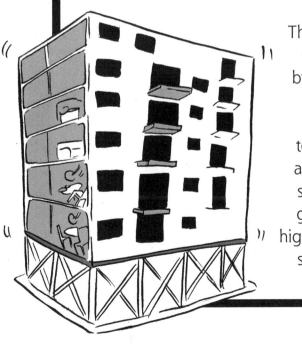

The E-Defense is an earthquake simulator with a shaking platform that is 50 feet by 60 feet (15 meters by 16 meters). The platform can support a structure that weighs over 1,300 tons (1,200 metric tons). That includes a full-scale house or a six-story, steel-reinforced building! The simulator replicates the same high-level ground movements that occur during a high-intensity earthquake, when the ground shakes both vertically and horizontally.

A Natural Building

SUPPLIES: *paper, pencil, ruler, natural materials (acorns, bark, leaves, moss, mud, pinecones, sand, rocks, sticks, etc.), tap water, tarp*

Ancient builders relied on materials found in nature to create their structures. Use natural elements to build your own structure, such as a footbridge or a tower. HINT: If your materials aren't solidly sticking together, try using more mud and wet sand for bonding.

1 Decide what you'd like to build. Use trial-and-error to sketch a design for a small tabletop structure. Include measurements for its height, width, and depth.

2 Gather up building materials found in nature, including those you can find from the ideas listed. Depending on where you live and the weather and climate, you'll find different materials. Have tap water available to keep mud and sand moist. They'll be more effective for making materials hold together.

3 Spread out the tarp. Now, use trial-and-error to follow the plans for your design. Working with different materials, arrange and manipulate them to build a sturdy structure. Discover which materials help other materials firmly stick together.

4 For each building material you use, make notes on the chart. Assess the pros and cons of the material.

5 Allow your structure to dry overnight. Then, test it out to see if it's holding securely. You might need to revisit some of your building materials to reinforce the structure.

Building Materials Assessment Chart

Material	Pros	Cons	Uses

TRY THIS

Extend the activity by building the same structure with a manmade building material such as modeling clay. How does the manmade material compare to the natural ones you used?

Egg Bungee Drop

SUPPLIES: *ziplock sandwich bag, paper puncher, large raw egg, large safety pin, 10 standard-sized rubber bands, scissors, old pair of tights or pantyhose, sticky note, marker, tape measure, footstool*

Zip your egg in a clear pouch and see if it can survive a wild ride. If it can't, use trial-and-error to make adjustments—and try, try again! HINT: You can substitute a hard-boiled egg to cut down on mess. Speaking of mess, the ziplock bag could burst, so you might want to conduct your experiment over a tarp or outside.

1 The ziplock sandwich bag is a harness for your egg. Punch a hole at the top of the bag. Open the ziplock and slip the egg inside. Then, open the safety pin, hook it through the hole, and close the pin with the top of the pin protruding from the bag. Carefully set the pouch aside for now.

2 Link the rubber bands to make a chain for the bungee cord. To start, weave one band inside of another and pull tightly to connect them. (Don't pull too tightly, though, or you'll snap them!) Add the rest of the rubber bands.

3 Open the safety pin and carefully attach one end of the rubber band chain to it. Close the pin. Cut off one leg from the tights or pantyhose. Securely tie it to the end of the rubber band chain.

4 Make an X on the sticky note with the marker. Use the tape measure to measure 40 inches up from the floor (about 100 centimeters). Attach the sticky note on the wall to mark the height you measured.

5 If you need to reach the marked height with a footstool, have an adult spot you while you step up. Hold the end of the tights or pantyhose, and drop the bungee from the marked height. See if your egg springs back without smashing.

6 If the egg doesn't survive, try the experiment again. What adjustments do you think you need to make to keep the egg intact? What do you predict would happen if you substituted a different elastic material for the tights?

Notable Quotable

"If we knew what we were doing, it wouldn't be called research, would it?"
—*Albert Einstein, Noble-Prize-winning physicist*
who developed the theory of relativity

What's the Strongest Shape?

SUPPLIES: *printer paper, clear tape, beverage can, paperback books*

Engineers use specific shapes to make structures strong and to evenly spread out the forces of compression and tension. Create some tents, upright triangles, and cylinders out of paper. Predict which structural shape will support the greatest number of books. Test out your prediction to discover how the shapes hold up under force.

1 Make a few of each shape first. Fold a sheet of paper in half horizontally and prop it on its bottom edges to make a tent.

2 For a triangle, fold one sheet of paper in thirds vertically. Tape the open edges together to hold the shape in place. Stand it up like a tower.

3 To make a cylinder, hold a sheet of paper vertically. Wrap the paper around the can, slip out the can, and tape the edges of the paper together.

4 Make sure all the shapes are placed on a stable surface. Predict what will happen when you place books on top of each shape. Which do you think will support the greatest number of books? Why?

5 Add one book at a time to each structural shape. Which immediately collapses under the weight? Which remains standing? Do all the shapes eventually collapse? What can you conclude about the ways the shapes spread out compression and tension?

BUILDING BIG: THE PHYSICS OF BRIDGES

A BRIDGE IS A STRUCTURE THAT SPANS AN OBSTACLE
such as a river or a road. Can you think of some bridges
made by nature? Trees topple across streams. Stone bridges
are carved by water and wind wearing away the rock.

NATURAL BRIDGES

Utah's Rainbow Bridge is the world's largest natural bridge. It towers 290 feet high (88 meters) and 270 feet wide (83 meters). Waters that flowed from the Navajo Mountains toward the Colorado River formed the curved sandstone bridge. This breathtaking natural wonder is a sacred place in Navajo and other Native American cultures.

MANMADE BRIDGES

The manmade bridge is one of the most important accomplishments in human engineering history. In 1931, President Franklin Delano Roosevelt gave a speech at the dedication of the George Washington Bridge in New York. He said, "There can be little doubt that in many ways the story of bridge building is the story of **civilization**. By it we can readily measure an important part of a people's progress."

Manmade bridges have existed since the first recorded history.

Early hunter-gatherers, walked great distances to find food, sources of fresh water, and fuel. When they encountered obstacles in their way, they found ways to bridge them.

Imagine a family living long ago. Perhaps they were traveling through woods from one seasonal village to another. One morning, they confronted a problem. They stumbled upon a stream too wide to leap across.

WORDS to KNOW

civilization: a community of people that is advanced in art, science, and government.

beam: a rigid horizontal structure that carries the load.

They scouted around for logs. One log was rotted, crumbling, and crawling with bugs. Another, solid and sturdy, was way too short. Finally, one of the kids found a long, hefty log. Working together, the family tackled different methods of positioning the log across the stream. Some squatted at the water's edge. Others took the plunge, swimming to maneuver the log in place.

Through creative thinking and trial-and-error, the family solved their problem. They built a primitive **beam** bridge and left it in place for others to use. Their ingenuity benefited people in their own village and travelers from other areas.

As human needs grew more complex, so did bridges.

• DID YOU KNOW?

Another meaning of bridge is "a link, connection, or way of coming together." People always explore innovative ways to "build bridges" with one another.

People erected bridges that seem crude today, but were ingenious for their time. They lugged granite slabs to creeks and piled them over rugged stones. They wove branches and twigs together and lashed them to two parallel logs. During times of peace, people built bridges for merchants to travel on foot or horseback hauling carts of goods to sell and trade. During times of war, armies built bridges so soldiers could attack enemy camps.

PHYSICS OF BRIDGES: A BALANCING ACT

Manmade bridges combine science and art. They serve a purpose, and at the same time can be beautiful. You've learned that structures must withstand forces. They need to stand up to the pull of gravity. All bridges have a **center of gravity** that keeps them balanced and stable. They rely on a balance of forces. So, how do bridges work? What keeps them from falling down?

Fierce waves, high winds, and natural disasters like earthquakes can batter bridges. In some climates, bridges go through extreme cycles of freezing and thawing each year. A bridge must also be strong enough to support the force of its own constant weight. This is **dead load**. It must support the changing weight of its **live load**.

WORDS to KNOW

center of gravity: the point on any object where all the weight is centered.

dead load: actual, constant weight of a structure.

live load: the changing weight of vehicles and pedestrians placed on a structure.

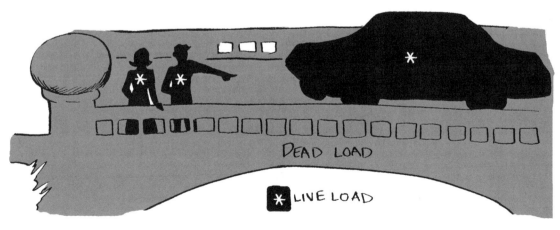

DEAD LOAD

* LIVE LOAD

Engineers use concepts of physical science to build bridges. They particularly use Newton's Third Law of Motion. That principle states, "For every action (force) there is an equal and opposite reaction (force)." Engineers design different types of bridges using mathematical calculations that consider the pulling force of tension and the opposite pushing force of compression.

If a bridge can't stand up to these forces it will buckle or snap.

After much careful study, engineers choose from three major bridge designs. These designs appear in bridges around the world. Each design handles tension and compression differently.

BRIDGES AS ART

Bridges are much more than calculations. Engineers consider the physical features of the area where a bridge will be built. "An element of beauty will come from the bridge's conformity to the environment," writes David Outerbridge in the book *Bridges*. Many bridges are works of art that have inspired poets, artists, novelists, composers, and movie scripts.

BEAM BRIDGE: SHORTEST SPANS

Like that log across the stream, the beam bridge is a simple, horizontal structure. Beam bridges are also called "**girder** bridges." They are typically the cheapest kind of bridge to build.

Its design uses clean lines. A beam bridge depends on two structures: the beam and **abutments**. The beam is a horizontal span, often made of concrete or steel. It's rigid to keep from twisting. Two vertical posts, or abutments, at opposite ends provide support. They support the bridge's constant dead load. They also bear the changing live load of vehicles traveling over it.

WORDS to KNOW

girder: a large beam, often made of steel.

abutment: a structure that supports a bridge, one at each end.

truss: a rigid framework of beams or bars that supports structures such as bridges.

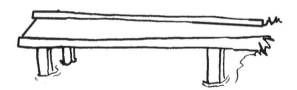

• DID YOU KNOW?

Engineering relies on triangles to construct **trusses**, a network of beams and bars. Trusses can be added above beam bridges or beneath their beams. They add support without adding excessive weight.

The beam and abutments are designed to withstand compression and tension. The beam pushes down on the abutments. If abutments are too far apart, there's a problem. The beam bends and weakens. Too much weight causes it to buckle and snap. That's why beam bridges span shorter distances than other bridges. They are usually no more than 250 feet long (76 meters).

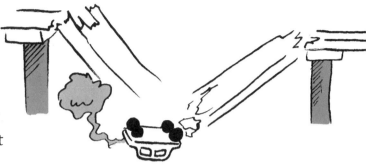

ARCH BRIDGE: LONGER SPANS

Arch bridges, in contrast, can be built over longer spans by using a series of arches. They generally span 200 to 800 feet (61 meters to 244 meters). The arch bridge is a curved, semicircular structure and one of the world's oldest designs. How does an arch stay standing? Its shape and the way it supports its load are the secret.

Arch bridges are also called "compression bridges."

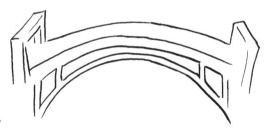

The arch bridge is naturally very strong. Like the beam bridge, an abutment at each end provides support. Because of their shape, arch bridges don't experience much tension, but they are always compressed. Unlike beam bridges, arch bridges don't push straight down. Instead, they work by transferring load weights along the curved area to the abutments. The abutments push against the arch, which keeps it from spreading apart.

SUSPENSION BRIDGE: LONGEST SPANS

Suspension bridges span the longest distances of all bridges. They span 2,000 to 8,000 feet (610 to 2440 meters) and are the most expensive to build.

A suspension bridge is an elegant design that sometimes looks so light it seems weightless.

But suspension bridges are deceptively sturdy. At opposite ends are **anchorages**. Like anchors on a ship, anchorages ground the bridge with their massive cables inside. Horizontal supporting cables run from anchorage to anchorage and are held up by huge towers spaced along the bridge. Strung vertically from the supporting cables are even more cables, or "hangers." A **deck** is suspended from the hangers.

Hangers transfer the weight of the load from the deck up to the supporting cables, which spread the bridge's tension along to the anchorages at each end. The anchorages send tension into the ground beneath them. The towers bear the compression forces that push down on the deck.

WORDS to KNOW

anchorage: a massive concrete slab driven into the earth to anchor, or ground, a suspension bridge.

deck: the roadway of a suspension bridge, which hangs from cables.

GEODESIC DOME

Architect, inventor, poet! Richard Buckminster Fuller (1895–1983), nicknamed Bucky, was a talented engineer. He devoted himself to helping others and finding ways to preserve resources. Fuller believed inexpensive designs could help people build comfortable, energy-efficient homes.

WORDS to KNOW

sphere: round, like a ball.
tetrahedron: a pyramid containing four triangular faces.

He challenged himself to "build a shelter so lightweight it can be delivered by air." In 1949, he built the world's first geodesic dome building. A geodesic dome structure is shaped like a **sphere**. Fuller used light plastics to form a series of **tetrahedrons**. These are pyramids with four triangular faces. Triangles are the strongest geometric shapes. Triangles stay stable because each side braces the two opposite sides, preventing them from moving in relation to each other.

His geodesic dome revolutionized engineering. It was the first building that could sustain its own weight without supports. When filled with air, geodesic domes weigh less than their own building materials!

Perhaps the world's most famous geodesic dome is Spaceship Earth at Epcot Theme Park in Orlando, Florida. It was built in partnership with Bucky Fuller, who coined the term "Spaceship Earth." He compared Earth to a spaceship journeying through space with all of humanity as passengers. He urged people to protect the earth's resources. Fuller was ahead of his time in looking for ways to create a sustainable future for the planet.

Marshmallow Geodesic Dome

SUPPLIES: *bag of mini marshmallows, box of toothpicks, books, scale*

Geodesic domes are structures made from a network of triangles. Build two domes out of toothpicks and marshmallows. Test how much weight in books they will support.

1 Connect 5 marshmallows with 5 toothpicks.

2 Start triangulating! Begin at one side of the base. Form a triangle out of 2 toothpicks with a marshmallow on top. The toothpicks should be angled toward each other, with the marshmallow connecting them. Work your way around the base's sections by constructing a triangle at each.

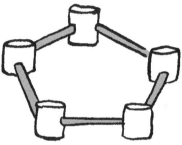

3 Use 5 toothpicks to connect each marshmallow in triangulated sections. These toothpicks should be arranged like the ones on the base.

4 Jab a toothpick into the top of the each of the five upper marshmallows. Angle them so they form a tent shape. Connect all of them by jabbing one final marshmallow over them.

5 Repeat the entire process to make your second dome. Let the domes dry overnight so the marshmallows harden.

6 Stand your domes side by side. Predict how many books they will support until they collapse. Add one book at a time. Observe what happens. Afterwards, weigh the books on a scale to figure out how much weight the domes could support.

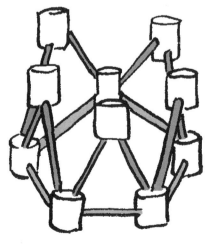

Beautiful Balancing Butterfly

SUPPLIES: *paper, pencil, scissors, file folder, colored markers, tape, 2 pennies, colored pencil, flat eraser*

Locate the center of gravity to create a butterfly that balances on your fingertip. HINT: Go to www.nomadpress.net/resources to download a template of the butterfly.

I Fold the paper in half. Draw half of the butterfly on the paper with the center of the butterfly on the fold. This way both sides of the butterfly will be the same. Cut out the pattern. Open it up and trace the whole butterfly onto the folder.

2 Be creative and decorate the butterfly with markers and then cut it out. Turn the butterfly over. In the exact same spot on the outer edge of each wing, tape a penny. These equal weights will allow the butterfly to balance. Make sure you use the same amount of tape with each penny because the tape has weight, too.

3 Move the butterfly's head around on your fingertip until you locate the center of gravity. You'll find it is probably near the front of the head. You'll know you've found it when the butterfly is balancing on your finger. If you can't get the butterfly to balance, use trial-and-error to move the pennies to a different spot on the wings and test the butterfly until you get it to balance.

4 Want to display your creation? Use a colored pencil for a stand. Make a platform out of a flat eraser. Jab the pointed end of the pencil into it. Balance your butterfly on the pencil's flat end. You can also try balancing the butterfly on other surfaces. Try the tip of your nose, the edge of a cup, or the corner of a table.

May the Force Be With You!

SUPPLIES: *2 empty paper towel tubes, scissors, shallow plastic tub, stable chair, duct tape, funnel, table salt, gravel, popcorn kernels, chart, pencil*

Immense girders support heavy loads on beam bridges. When a load presses on girders, it causes compression. For a bridge to stay standing, the girders must tolerate that compression. Building materials affect the strength of structures. Can you stand on different paper-tube girders without squishing them under the compression forces of your body weight?

1 Cut both tubes in half so you have four tubes of equal size. Test an empty tube first. Place the plastic tub next to the chair. Position the tube so it's laying like a girder inside the tub. Predict what will happen when you stand on top of the tube. Have someone spot you or hold the chair for support. Slowly stand with one foot on the tube. Little by little, allow more of your body weight to press down on it. What happens?

2 Build the second girder using table salt and duct tape. Completely seal one end of the tube with tape. Using the funnel, pour salt into the other end until the tube is filled. Seal the open end with tape. Gently shake the tube to make sure there are no holes. If there is a hole, apply more tape. Predict what will happen when you press your weight on the tube. Repeat the compression process using a spotter or a chair for support.

3 Build a third girder using another tube. Seal one end with tape. Use the funnel to fill the tube with gravel. Tape the other end shut. Check for holes, make your prediction, and repeat the compression process.

4 Build the final girder, this time using popcorn kernels. Repeat the process. Seal the tube, check for holes, make a prediction, and test the compression.

5 Complete the chart with a description of what took place during each test. Explain which tubes collapsed. What conclusions can you draw about the strength of different construction materials? How can various materials be used to impact strength?

Empty Tube	Salt Tube	Gravel Tube	Popcorn
Prediction:	Prediction:	Prediction:	Prediction:
What Happened:	What Happened:	What Happened:	What Happened:
Conclusion:	Conclusion:	Conclusion:	Conclusion:

Parachute Plunge

SUPPLIES: *keychain toy, stopwatch, scissors, empty plastic grocery bag, tape measure or ruler, yarn*

Take the plunge, and defy gravity! Can you build a parachute that withstands gravitational pull?

1 When you drop something, it speeds toward Earth. That's the pull of gravity. Stand up, hold the toy in one hand, and extend your arm. Have a friend use the stopwatch to time how long it takes the toy to hit the ground when you drop it.

WORDS to KNOW

gravitational pull: the pull of objects to the surface of the earth.

2 A parachute slows down the speed of the toy's drop as it plunges toward Earth. To build a parachute, cut the handles off the plastic bag. Measure a 14-by-14-inch square area on the bag (36½ centimeters square). Cut it out. Keep the bottom of the bag intact.

Notable Quotable

"I know this defies the law of gravity, but I never studied law."
—*Bugs Bunny, cartoon trickster and goofball*

3 Tie a knot in each of the four corners. Measure and cut five 12-inch lengths of yarn (30½ centimeters). Set one aside. Tie each of the other pieces tightly around one of the four knots on the corners.

4 To make a harness, gather the four pieces of yarn and knot them together. Loop the remaining piece of string through the top of the keychain. Then tie the keychain to the large knot you made from the four strings. Let the toy dangle from the harness.

5 Test your chute! Predict whether it will end in a crash landing or drift gently to the ground. Lightly grasp the outside of the chute at the center. Toss it high overhead. You should see the parachute billow out as it traps air. While air pushes against the chute, gravity continues to pull it down. Because of air resistance, the toy should have a slower plunge to Earth than it did without the parachute. Use the stopwatch to time how long it takes the toy to land with the parachute. How do the results differ from your earlier test?

 **• DID YOU KNOW?**

Bridges are BATS! BATS is an acronym, which is a word formed from initials. BATS is a word formed from the first initials of the words **B**eams, **A**rches, **T**russes, and **S**uspension.

Soda Can Rocket

SUPPLIES: *3 bright stickers, 3 empty soft drink cans with pull tabs in place, permanent marker, 3 carpenter's nails of different sizes, ruler, scissors, string, large tub filled with water, towels*

Use action-reaction thrust to set this rocket into rotating motion— Newton's Third Law of Motion! Thrust is the reactive force generated by a rocket or jet engine. HINT: You might want to take this activity outdoors and try it over a kiddie pool filled with water!

1 Place one sticker on the side of each can. These markers will help later when you count how many times each can rotates. With the marker, label the bottom of each can with the number 1, 2, or 3.

2 Ask an adult to help you pierce the cans. With the smallest nail, make four punctures equally around can 1 near the bottom. Wriggle the nail to the right to make each hole angled. This will allow water to stream out at an angle, which will produce the thrust needed to set the rockets in motion. With the medium nail, do the same for can 2. With the largest nail, do the same for can 3.

3 Measure and cut three lengths of string, each 10 inches long (25½ centimeters). Tie one piece to each pull-tab on the cans.

4 Test each can in turn by plunging it into the tub. Allow the can to completely fill with water. Then remove it and dangle it from the string over the tub. Water gushing from holes will create thrust. Count the number of rotations each can makes. What conclusions can you draw about how the size of the nail holes affects the number of rotations?

AMAZING BRIDGES

FROM ANCIENT ARCH BRIDGES STILL USED TODAY TO FAMOUS bridges on the East and West coasts of the United States and around the world, bridges span the ages. They are monuments to creativity and ingenuity.

ROMAN ARCH BRIDGES

The Roman Empire existed between 752 BCE and 476 CE. The expert bridge-builders of ancient Rome created magnificent arch bridges throughout Europe, Asia, and Africa. Roman engineers constructed roads to move its mighty armies to faraway battlefields.

Once the Romans conquered an area, they constructed new cities. Roman engineers got to work building stone arch bridges. Stone was heavy and tough to work with, but that also made it a sturdy building material. It could hold up against any weather without rotting like wood.

To begin building a stone arch, **laborers** put up a curved wooden frame. Like a skeleton, the temporary frame formed the bridge's bones. Starting at each end, laborers placed stones over the frame. Because of the curved arch shape, **mortar** wasn't needed to hold the stones in place. Wedged tightly where the arch's two curves met at the top, was a **keystone** that joined the sides together. This was the stone that locked the arch in place. With compression forces at work, the arch's bridge remained stable and could support extremely heavy loads.

WORDS to KNOW

laborer: someone who does physical work using his or her hands.

mortar: a mixture of cement, sand, and water that dries hard like stone. It is like glue holding bricks or stones together.

keystone: a wedge-shaped stone that locks the two sections of a Roman arch in place.

DID YOU KNOW?

Like the wooden frames the Romans used, workers today use temporary framework structures called falsework. These support building or railway construction sites while they are built.

ZHAOZHOU BRIDGE

Li Chun built China's Zhaozhou Bridge, which spans the Jiao River, around 595 CE. Amazingly preserved, it has endured repeated earthquakes and floods. The single-arch stone bridge is a treasured work of art. Detailed carved dragons and lotus flowers decorate its stone posts. Carved in the center is a water dragon, which protects the river from drought. The beloved bridge remains in use today.

PONTE FABRICIO: ROME, ITALY

- **TYPE:** Stone double-arch bridge
- **TOTAL SPAN:** 203 feet (62 meters)
- **SPANS:** Tiber River to The Tiber Island (Isola Tiberina)
- **CONSTRUCTION DATE:** 62 BCE

Roman arch bridges are such astonishing feats of engineering that some have survived for over 2,000 years and are still in use today. In 62 BCE, Lucius Fabricus built the Pons Fabricus, now called Ponte Fabricio, in Rome. The bridge is incredibly well preserved. It is Rome's oldest bridge, and the only one still in its original state. The bridge boasts two 90-foot-tall arches (27½ meters). It provides access from the left bank of the Tiber River to The Tiber Island, a small island in the middle of the river, shaped like a ship. Engineers designed two curved arches high enough to allow ship traffic to sail beneath the bridge.

WORDS to KNOW

pile driver: a large machine that pushes posts into the ground.

barge: a boat with a flat bottom used to carry loads.

pulley: a simple machine consisting of a wheel with a grooved rim that a rope or chain is pulled through to help lift up a load.

EXTREME ENGINEERING

In 55 BCE, Julius Caesar ruled the Roman Empire. His engineers used an early **pile driver** to construct a wooden beam bridge that spanned the Rhine River in present-day Germany. They hauled the large mechanical device on a **barge**. To use the pile driver, laborers lifted a heavy stone with a **pulley**. They released the stone on top of pointy oak timbers that rammed into the ground beneath the river. Laborers strengthened the bridge so it could stand up to powerful currents. According to Caesar's writings, construction took only 10 days!

THE BROOKLYN BRIDGE: NEW YORK, UNITED STATES

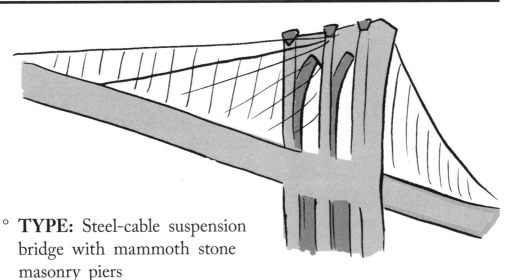

- **TYPE:** Steel-cable suspension bridge with mammoth stone masonry piers
- **TOWER HEIGHT:** 277 feet (84 meters)
- **TOTAL SPAN:** 5,989 feet (1,825 meters), or 1.13 miles (1.82 kilometers)
- **SPANS:** East River to connect Manhattan and Brooklyn
- **CONSTRUCTION DATES:** 1869–1883

Water surrounds Manhattan in New York, the United States' largest city. Before the Brooklyn Bridge was built, ferry boats on the East River carried people between Manhattan and Brooklyn. Cargo ships jammed the river. The river's waters could be rough and often froze in the winter. New Yorkers demanded a bridge to make travel easier between Brooklyn and Manhattan. And it needed to be high enough to allow ship traffic to sail beneath it.

If you've ever seen the Brooklyn Bridge, you know it was an incredible feat of engineering.

Several members of the Roebling family worked on the construction of the Brooklyn Bridge. John Augustus Roebling was a brilliant civil engineer from Germany. He **pioneered** the use of steel in bridge building. Roebling invented a technique to twist many steel wires into rope. Strong **suspension cables** could be made from the steel rope.

Roebling believed that steel was the ideal material for the Brooklyn Bridge. He argued that with the strength of steel, bridges could span longer distances than ever before. Steel suspension bridges, though light, could support heavier loads than other bridges.

Roebling was determined to build an elegant structure with two dramatic **Gothic** arches. One night, he was standing at the edge of the water puzzling over how to engineer the beautiful bridge he wanted. He was writing down detailed mathematical calculations for where to place the towers. Suddenly, a ferry came speeding toward him and hit him. He died a few weeks later from his injuries.

DID YOU KNOW?

There are more suspension bridges in the United States than in the rest of the world combined!

Fortunately, his son, Washington Roebling, was an accomplished bridge builder. After his father's death, Washington Roebling became the Brooklyn Bridge's chief engineer. But like his father, the project proved disastrous to his health.

Construction began in 1870. It required using wooden **caissons**. Builders used these 3,000-ton devices to secure towers deep underground, under the river. The caissons were enormous airtight, watertight chambers with a closed top and an open bottom. The chamber was lowered into position at the bottom of the river. Crews of men were lowered into the chamber each day where they worked using hand picks and shovels to dig out the mud and sediment from the mucky riverbed.

WORDS to KNOW

caisson: a watertight structure filled with air under pressure. It is used for underwater construction.

GEORGE WASHINGTON BRIDGE

With 12 traffic lanes on its upper level and 12 on its lower, the George Washington Bridge is one of the world's busiest. Between anchorages, the suspension bridge is 4,760 feet long (1,451 meters). Spanning the Hudson River, it connects Manhattan in New York with New Jersey. In 2009, according to the Port Authority of New York and New Jersey, 52,126,000 vehicles motored across the bridge. Eastbound!

45

CAISSON'S DISEASE

Workers in the caisson were called sandhogs. They earned $2 a day for high-risk, backbreaking labor in horrendous working conditions. To keep the chamber dry, engineers pumped in **compressed air**. This created so much pressure inside the chamber that it kept the surrounding water out. Otherwise, the pressure from the water would burst the caissons and the sandhogs would drown. But compressed air made the caissons extremely dangerous—and broiling hot. The men worked in constant fear. They slogged through awful-smelling muck. They strained their eyes in the deep, dark surroundings lit by dim gaslights.

To exit pressurized compartments, workers crept up through **air locks**. Surfacing too quickly was extremely dangerous. In the late 1800s, little was known about how **decompression** impacted the body. But it causes sickness and sometimes even death. Many men experienced unbearable chest pains, dizziness, and even paralysis. This is the loss of the ability to move a part of the body. They called this illness "caisson's disease." Today it's known as decompression sickness, or "the bends."

WORDS to KNOW

compressed air: air that is under more pressure than the outside air.

air lock: an airtight chamber between two areas of unequal pressure, in which air pressure can be controlled.

decompression: a drop in water pressure.

DID YOU KNOW?

Granite sometimes fell from the structure, crushing bridgemen working on towers and wires. Others blew off the bridge during heavy winds. In all, about 40 workers lost their lives during the project.

Eventually the workers reached the solid **bedrock** that would provide a stable base for the bridge and could stop digging. Once the men and their equipment were lifted out, the caissons were filled with concrete. Above the surface of the water, **stonemasons** stacked layers of stones on top of the caissons.

WORDS to KNOW

bedrock: the solid rock that lies beneath loose material, such as soil, sand, clay, or gravel.

stonemason: a person who is skilled in building with stone.

In this way, gigantic towers were constructed to support the bridge.

During construction of the bridge, engineers pumped compressed air into the caissons to keep water from rushing in from the outside. The compressed air created too much pressure inside the caisson for the water to break through. As digging continued, the gloomy, pressurized caissons plunged lower and lower into the riverbed. The deeper the caissons sank, the greater the water pressure from outside became. This meant that the pressure of the compressed air had to get stronger and stronger to keep the water out.

Sometimes blowouts occurred when compressed air found a way to escape beneath caissons. One blowout created a waterspout almost 600 feet high (183 meters). Others blew men up in the air to their deaths.

In an 1870 fire in the Brooklyn caisson, Roebling worked to extinguish the blaze. He spent too much time in the compressed and smoke-filled air, and suffered an attack of the bends. It left him paralyzed for hours. By 1872, he fell seriously ill after another attack. In agony, the engineer could barely hold up his own weight.

• DID YOU KNOW?

The Brooklyn Bridge was once nicknamed the eighth wonder of the world. In 1883, it was the longest, heaviest suspension bridge ever built. Crews bundled 100 wires into each strand of cable. They used over 80,000 miles of pencil-thin wire (129,000 kilometers). That's enough to wind more than three times around the earth and still tie a bow!

Deaf, partially blind, and paralyzed from the waist down, Washington Roebling was confined to his bed. But he was not defeated. From a Brooklyn Heights apartment near the river, he would peer through a telescope to keep an eye on the construction.

Once more, the baton passed—this time to Roebling's wife. For the next 11 years, Emily Warren Roebling supervised construction at the site. Emily Roebling was a pioneer. Considered the United States' first female field engineer, she managed bridge construction at a time when women rarely worked outside the home.

NIAGARA RIVER SUSPENSION BRIDGE

One of the earliest wire cable suspension bridges opened in 1848 over the Niagara River, near the famous Niagara Falls. It connected Niagara Falls in Ontario, Canada, to Niagara Falls in New York. Civil engineer Charles Ellet, Jr., managed the construction. In the middle of a frigid winter, he faced his first obstacle. And it was huge—a chasm 800 feet wide (244 meters) and 200 feet deep (61 meters). It was also treacherous. Steep, rocky walls surrounded the yawning gorge. Violent rapids churned in the waters beneath it.

How could Ellet get a suspension line, the first step in the building process, to the other side? He thought of blasting it over with a rocket. He contemplated tying it to a bombshell and exploding it from a cannon. Finally, Ellet challenged boys in the area to fly kites over the river. Engineers offered a cash prize to the first boy whose kite survived. Fifteen-year-old Homan Walsh battled bone-chilling weather and succeeded. Once Ellet knew that a kite worked, he used one to fly a cable across the chasm. A marvel of engineering was underway.

To advance the enormous project, Emily Roebling studied civil engineering and math. She scoured books about the strength of different building materials. She dug into information about cable construction.

As the technical leader and chief engineer, she visited the work site each day.

DID YOU KNOW?

The Brooklyn Bridge's main suspension cables begin and end on land. They drape gracefully over the tower at the middle of the span and again at a second tower. An arch at the south end adds to the grandeur. Architects included the arch to save Fort Point, a Civil War fort, from the wrecker's ball! They preserved the historic site.

Some people grumbled that with a woman overseeing construction, the bridge would not be well built and would be unsafe to use. Emily Roebling responded by demonstrating the bridge's safety herself. When the Brooklyn Bridge officially opened in 1883, she was the first to cross it. Schools and shops closed so crowds could cheer the festivities. As they watched, a horse galloped across the span pulling Emily Roebling in an elegant carriage. In her arms, she held a crowing rooster as a symbol of victory.

With a fireworks celebration that dazzled thousands, the Brooklyn Bridge opened to the public. President Chester A. Arthur strolled across the bridge with huge crowds watching from both sides of the river. That evening, Emily Roebling hosted a grand party in her husband's honor.

Today, the Brooklyn Bridge is a National Historic Civil Engineering Landmark. A plaque on the bridge honors Emily Warren Roebling, her husband, Washington Roebling, and her father-in-law, John Augustus Roebling.

THE GOLDEN GATE BRIDGE: SAN FRANCISCO, CALIFORNIA, UNITED STATES

- **TYPE:** Steel-cable suspension bridge with two main towers
- **TOWER HEIGHT:** 746 feet (227 meters)
- **TOTAL LENGTH:** 8,981 feet (2,737 meters), or 1.7 miles (2.75 kilometers)
- **SPANS:** Golden Gate inlet between San Francisco and the Pacific Ocean
- **CONSTRUCTION DATES:** 1933–1937

As the port city of San Francisco, California, boomed in the 1920s, traffic exploded. Motorists clogged congested streets. Commuters crammed ferries to cross the wide and dangerous San Francisco Bay to suburbs outside the city. Ferry lines seemed endless. Frazzled commuters were trapped in cars as long as 18 hours. As they had in New York, people rallied for new bridges to get them where they needed to go. Bridges would provide shorter routes and speedier journeys. They would ease congestion.

The Golden Gate is an inlet, a narrow stretch of water between San Francisco Bay and the Pacific Ocean. It presented a unique engineering challenge. Its turbulent winds, churning waves, and dense fog are famous. Worse, it sprawls between the Hayward and San Andreas **fault zones**, near the epicenter of the San Francisco Earthquake of 1906. This earthquake killed 3,000 people and was the most disastrous quake in United States history.

WORDS to KNOW

rivet: a short metal pin or bolt for holding together two plates of metal.

fault zone: an area that is at risk of earthquakes.

Could any bridge possibly stand up to a similar catastrophe?

United States' engineers had never before constructed a bridge like it. Engineer Joseph B. Strauss got to work. He planned a marvel over the misty bay that would stand 4,200 feet high (1,280 meters) and 90 feet wide (27 meters). A suspension bridge high enough to accommodate waves at high tide turned out to be the ideal design for the wide span of water.

WORDS to KNOW

Great Depression: a time in United States history when the economy struggled and many people lost their money, homes, and jobs.

cofferdam: a temporary watertight structure pumped dry and used for underwater construction.

Construction began in 1933 during the **Great Depression**. Divers plunged into the chilly bay. They built a **cofferdam** for laborers to work underwater. With jackhammers and steam shovels, they dug down to bedrock. They poured concrete under water to lay foundations. Onshore, workers blasted explosives. They dug up rock to build piers. Within two years, the world's largest steel towers, weighing 22,000 tons, stood like giants out of the bay.

Next, Strauss planned to hang suspension cables. All the weight of the bridge would hang from these cables. The bridge's weight, plus the weight of car traffic, would press straight down on the floor of the bridge and cause compression. The cables would spread out the weight. But hanging the cables across the structure was the tricky part.

Strauss employed the renowned Roebling Engineering Company from New York to handle the cable construction. Crews used Roebling's famous technique of twisting steel wires into rope strands. Bridgemen balanced on beams at dizzying heights of up to 746 feet over the bay (227 meters). A blinding jolt of sunlight could cause a disastrous false step. A gust of wind might toss a worker into the waters below with the force of a car bashing into a brick wall at 80 miles per hour (129 kilometers per hour). But fortunately, Joseph Strauss was a pioneer of worker safety. He hung a gigantic safety net like those used in acrobatic acts beneath the beams. The ingenious idea saved many bridgemen who toppled from their **precarious** perches.

WORDS to KNOW

precarious: in danger of falling or collapsing.

corrode: to rust.

Strauss's bridgemen were the first to wear hard hats and goggles on a construction job.

DON'T JUMP JOE.

BUT THE OTHER GUYS SAID IT WAS FUN!

After four years of construction, the bridge opened in 1937. In a huge celebration called Pedestrian Day, a cheering crowd of 30,000 people paid a nickel each to walk the span of the bridge. Today, the iconic Golden Gate Bridge still looks sleek, elegant, and strong. It's painted "vermillion orange" or "international orange." The burnt orange color blends with the bay's stunning natural landscape. Painting the bridge is an ongoing, important part of its upkeep. The paint protects it from San Francisco's harsh weather conditions and salty sea air, which **corrode** steel. And the bridge stands out against the gray fog, which helps ships avoid collision.

Millions of tourists flock to visit the Golden Gate Bridge every year. Views are especially breathtaking at sunset.

WONDROUS BRIDGES 'ROUND THE WORLD

ARENAL HANGING BRIDGE (Arenal Volcanic National Park, Costa Rica, 2004)

- ° Pedestrian, steel suspension bridge spans the rain forest with six individual bridges from 157 to 321 feet (48–98 meters).

- ° Slung above the rainforest's lush canopy, it offers hikers a birds-eye view of the volcano.

BOSPHORUS BRIDGE (Istanbul, Turkey, 1974)

- ° Steel suspension bridge spans the Bosphorus Straits to link the continents of Europe and Asia: 3,524 feet (1,074 meters).

- ° Eurasia Marathon runners span two continents when they race across the bridge every October. The race celebrates peace and friendship.

KHAJU BRIDGE (Isfahan, Iran, 1667)

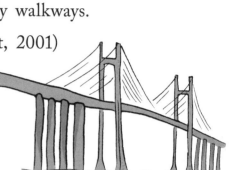

○ Stone and brick arch bridge spans the Zayandeh River: 344 feet (105 meters).

○ Covered in brightly colored tiles and adorned with seventeenth-century artwork, it boasts a magnificent pavilion and cool, shady walkways.

SUEZ CANAL BRIDGE (El Qantara, Egypt, 2001)

○ World's highest cable-stayed suspension bridge spans Suez Canal to link the continents of Africa and Asia: 120 miles (193 kilometers).

○ Also called the Egyptian-Japanese Friendship Bridge, it has obelisk-shaped towers to honor the achievements of ancient Egyptian kings.

SYDNEY HARBOR BRIDGE (Sydney, Australia, 1939)

○ World's largest steel arch bridge spans Sydney Harbor: 3,769 feet (1,149 meters).

○ Catwalks, ladders, and stairs! Adventurers love to climb to the summit, 440 feet above sea level (134 meters). Locals nicknamed the bridge the "Coat Hanger" because of its curved shape.

YONGLE BRIDGE (Tianjin, China, 2007)

○ Cement and steel beam bridge spans the Hai River: 410 feet (125 meters).

○ This is the world's only bridge with an attached, 360-foot high Ferris wheel (110 meters). Called the Tianjin Eye, it seats 384 dangling skyriders!

Geometric Shape Mosaic

SUPPLIES: *dried pumpkin seeds in shells, wax paper, different colored paints, paint brushes, paper, colored pencils, ceramic tile, glue*

A mosaic is a design or picture made with tiles or stones. Iran's spectacular Khaju Bridge is decorated with dazzling tiles. Make a mosaic tile using geometric shapes and patterns.

1 Spread the seeds over a sheet of wax paper. Paint all the seeds, front and back, using a variety of colors. Let the seeds dry completely.

2 While the seeds dry, sketch a geometric design out of shapes on paper. Use the colored pencils to fill in areas of the design with the colors you'll use in your mosaic.

3 Once the seeds have dried, arrange them on the tile according to your design. Use glue to secure them to the tile and to one another. Allow your tile to dry completely.

DID YOU KNOW?

Michael Williams of Shoebury, England, used 1.6 million wooden matches to construct a dazzling replica of London's Tower Bridge. It took 10 years to complete. That's two years longer than it took to build the actual suspension bridge!

Craft Stick Beam Bridge

SUPPLIES: *wax paper, jumbo wooden craft sticks, wood glue, 2 hardcover books, metal binder clips, wood blocks, weights to test the bridge*

Engineers rely on triangular shapes as bridge supports. Strong and rigid, the triangle is the most stable shape. Compression at one joint is balanced by tension across the opposite side. Construct a simple beam bridge with triangular trusses. Will it support a heavy load? HINT: Need an extra set of hands? Ask a friend to help you!

1 Spread out the wax paper for a work surface. Count out 14 craft sticks. Lay the sticks flat side-by-side. Glue them together along their long edges to build a deck that spans 12 inches (30 centimeters). Place one book at each end to keep the deck flat and in place while it dries. Allow the deck to dry completely, checking occasionally to make sure it doesn't stick to the wax paper.

2 Count out eight more craft sticks. With four sticks, construct two angled braces across the deck by forming them into a "V" shape. Glue them in place. Then place a stick horizontally across the pointed end and the open end of each "V". Glue them in place. Secure the sticks with binder clips and allow the braces to dry completely.

3 Count out four more craft sticks. Turn the deck over so the braces are on the back. Turn two sticks on their edges so the wider sides are facing you. Glue them to the bottom of the deck, along the horizontal sticks you added in step one. Press them between books until they dry. Repeat on the other opposite edge.

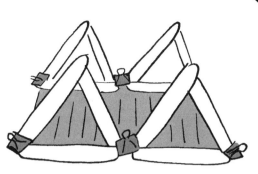

4 Count out six more sticks. Construct a triangular truss over half of one side of the deck. Angle one stick so it touches the end of the sideways stick you added in step three. Angle a second stick so it touches the opposite end. Glue the bottoms to the sideways stick. Use another sideways stick. Glue it to the back of the two bottoms. Secure with clips in both places. The two angled sticks should be sandwiched between the two sideways sticks. Don't glue the point of the triangle together. Repeat to make a second triangular truss next to the first. Then make two triangular trusses on the other side of the deck in the same way. Allow the trusses to dry completely.

5 Hold another stick sideways with the wider side facing you. Starting with the two trusses on one side of the deck, position the stick between the two angled sticks at the top of each triangle. Glue the stick in place and secure them with clips while they dry. Repeat on the other side of the deck. Allow the glue to dry completely.

6 Use three more sticks. To support the top of the bridge, position two sticks flat across the tops of each end of the trusses. Position another stick in the center. Glue all the sticks in place and clip the center stick in place. Allow the bridge to dry overnight.

7 Check to see if there are any sections that didn't firmly glue together. Re-glue and clamp them until they are dry. When everything is dry and holding in place, test the weight the bridge will support. Prop the bridge between wood blocks. Start with something light. Place the load on the deck. Gradually increase the weight of the load. How much weight will the bridge withstand before it collapses? How could you modify the design of the bridge so it will support heavier loads? Build another bridge with your new ideas.

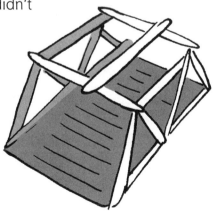

Sugar Cube Arch

SUPPLIES: *measuring tape, sheet of aluminum foil 20 inches by 8 inches (50 by 20 centimeters), 15-ounce can of soup or beans (425 grams), box of sugar cubes, Elmer's glue, mini spatula or cotton swabs, 2 hardcover books, emery board or nail file*

Build an arch around a false frame like the Romans did! Can it resist collapse? HINT: This arch is not edible.

1 Fold the foil in half lengthwise, so it measures 20 inches by 4 inches (50 by 10 centimeters). Set the can on its side and arrange the foil over it into an arch shape for support during construction. Leave two 3-inch by 4-inch flat areas of foil at either side (7½ by 12½ centimeters).

2 Build the side columns first, working on top of the flat areas of foil on the ends. Build parallel, horizontal rows of sugar-cube bricks. Be sure each row uses the same number of cubes. Use glue as mortar. Work it into place with the spatula or swabs. The trick is to add glue in the right places. Cubes should stick to the foil and to each another. Trial-and-error will help you figure out the best method. For the sturdiest arch and to avoid collapse during construction, allow each layer to dry before you build the next on top. Prop books at either side to support the cubes as they dry.

Notable Quotable

"Creativity is contagious. Pass it on."
—*Albert Einstein*

3 Next, start gluing cubes up the foil until you reach the area where the arch starts to curve. Locate the center of the arch. Build a horizontal row of cubes across it the short way. After the row dries, build another to the right and left of it. Make sure the cubes that form the arch are attached to one another and to the side columns.

4 Use the emery board to sand each cube into place. You'll probably find trapezoidal shapes work well. Shape a keystone to wedge the sides in place.

5 Allow your arch to dry completely overnight. Lie it on its side to slip the can out. Carefully turn the arch upright. Does it stand up or collapse?

TRY THIS

You can also build the arch in a flat position, without a false frame. Form the sides and top on a sheet of foil or wax paper. File sugar cubes into shape as necessary. Glue them in place. Place the can in the center for support. Allow the arch to harden overnight. The next day, carefully lift it to an upright position. Which method worked better?

DISASTER! WHEN BRIDGES COLLAPSE

TSUNAMIS, HURRICANES, AND TORNADOES . . .
landslides, floods, and earthquakes. Massive bridges
tower like steel giants. Yet, the forces of nature
make them as vulnerable as a house of cards.

Trains and ships crash into bridges. Tension forces take them down. Bridges fail under structural problems, overload, design flaws, and poor building materials. Throughout history, bridges have collapsed causing death and injury to people and animals. They have destroyed vehicles and damaged the environment.

IRON: REVOLUTIONARY BUILDING MATERIAL

For centuries, bridge builders relied on stone. The stonework looked beautiful, but it was heavy, expensive, and cumbersome. Engineers wanted a replacement material with stone's strength that was less expensive and easier to use.

In 1779, an English engineer named Abraham Darby built the arched Iron Bridge with a revolutionary material called **cast iron**. Cast iron is as strong as stone and can withstand great weight. It is also less expensive and easier to build with than stone. Previously, workers pounded hot iron into shape with hammers. But cast iron is shaped by "casting" **molten** iron into long, strong molds. To construct Darby's structure, crews melted the iron in blast furnaces and cast it into a variety of shapes and sizes.

WORDS to KNOW

cast iron: a hard, brittle type of iron that lends itself to casting rather than pounding.

molten: turned into liquid through heat.

DID YOU KNOW?

Ironworkers cast the Iron Bridge's arch ribs in just two pieces. Each massive rib weighed 6 tons. That's about the weight of six sports cars!

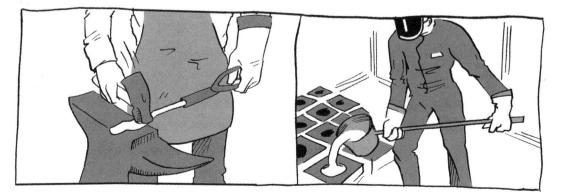

WORDS to KNOW

prefabricated: made in pieces or sections, then put together at a construction site.

wrought iron: an iron that can be worked when it is hot. It is not brittle like cast iron.

Spanning the River Severn, Great Britain's longest river, the Iron Bridge measured 100 feet long (30 meters). Construction of the world's first cast iron bridge changed building methods. Bridges became huge puzzles assembled with **prefabricated** pieces.

People hailed the Iron Bridge as a momentous achievement. Unfortunately, cast iron is brittle and can snap. Even worse, it can't be bent or shaped after it has cooled. Hammering on red hot, even white hot, cast iron will just break it. It has caused collapse in more than one bridge disaster.

In his book, *Engineers of Dreams: Great Bridge Builders and the Spanning of America*, Henry Petroski wrote, "Increasing use of iron in bridges of ever-greater spans led to increasingly innovative and daring designs . . ." But, repeatedly, these iron bridges resulted in "colossal failure" and collapsed.

Notable Quotable

"Under wrong conditions cast iron buckles and breaks … **Wrought iron** performs best under tension as a floor beam, while cast iron performs best under compression, as a column. Nobody really understood these distinctions when builders began putting up iron bridges."
—*Jim Rasenberger, author of* High Steel

LONDON BRIDGE

"London Bridge is falling down, Falling down, Falling down . . ."

Does this rhyme sound familiar? Children around the world chant it. And its words ring true! London Bridge was originally a crude Roman bridge built in 52 CE. The bridge spanned the River Thames in England for centuries. But it fell down. Many times.

From the years 1000 to 1300, war, wind, fire, and ice caused collapse. In 1014, warriors ripped it down. King Olaf flattened it during a Viking naval battle. In 1091, weather collapsed the rickety timber bridge. Later a tornado's violent winds battered the structure. Londoners patched it up with "sticks." Flames destroyed it next. Especially vulnerable to fires, the bridge burned down around 1135. A devastating blaze ravaged the entire city. In time, people rebuilt both London and their beloved bridge.

In 1176, Peter de Colechurch, a parish priest, designed a more permanent structure. He planned a stone bridge with 19 arches. By 1209, de Colechurch's redesigned London Bridge was complete. Within the century, though, winter weather crushed it. In 1281, the River Thames froze over and expanding ice demolished five of the bridge's arches. Once more, London Bridge went falling down.

THE DEE BRIDGE DISASTER, 1847

In 1847, England was in the middle of the **Industrial Revolution**. This meant that bridges needed to support heavy steam engines known as "iron horses" weighing up to 60 tons. One of England's first railway disasters revealed cast iron's fatal flaw. Tension's pulling force caused **structural collapse**.

One day in May, six trains raced safely across the Dee Bridge. The small beam bridge spanned the River Dee near Chester, England. Robert Stephenson had constructed the bridge on trussed, cast iron girders. Ironworkers built each girder from three iron castings joined together. Later that evening, a seventh train, weighing 60 tons and traveling 30 miles per hour (48 kilometers per hour), sped toward catastrophe. When one girder couldn't stand up to the tension forces, it became brittle, fractured, and buckled.

WORDS to KNOW

Industrial Revolution: a period of time beginning in the late 1700s when people started using machines to make things in large factories.

structural collapse: failure of a building, bridge, tower, or other structure.

DID YOU KNOW?

Seismic engineers recently conducted a seismic retrofit project on the Golden Gate Bridge. Using new insights about earthquakes and seismic movement, they modified support towers. They adjusted the Fort Point Arch, anchorages, and pylons to stand up to earthquakes. The project increased safety without altering the structure's iconic architecture.

The Illustrated London News reported that the engineer driver, "felt rails sinking beneath him, and he instantly put on steam." The engine "cleared the bridge and reached abutments" but it couldn't halt disaster. Beneath the locomotive's crushing weight, the horizontal structure ripped apart. Tracks rippled like bent cardboard, throwing the train right off the rails.

The bridge collapsed. Train carriages filled with passengers plunged into the water. Debris from the collapsed structure rained on them. Five people, including a young stoker who fed coal into the engine, lost their lives. Thirteen were critically injured.

Investigators blamed the catastrophe on structural collapse. After the disaster, engineers discovered that wrought iron and steel could resist tension forces better than cast iron. The rebuilt Dee Bridge was constructed of wrought iron. They achieved another major stride in bridge-building knowledge, but sadly it was at the expense of human life.

TACOMA NARROWS BRIDGE

In 1940, torsion's twisting force caused failure of the Tacoma Narrows Bridge over Puget Sound in Washington State. Held up as a modern wonder, the bridge was light and slim. At the time, it was the third-longest suspension span in the world, behind the George Washington and Golden Gate bridges. With a steel and concrete deck, slender spans, and a girder instead of a truss, it was extremely flexible.

Laborers who constructed the bridge were called "boomers." One boomer nicknamed the bridge "Galloping Gertie" because of the way its span bounced up and down. Gertie collapsed a mere four months after opening. Strong, 40-mile-per-hour winds caused the bridge's deck to ripple up-and-down and side-to-side like a party streamer. Suspension cables twisted. Towers bent. The deck's movement caused a **vortex**. Swirling wind raised and twisted the deck even more violently. The twisting became so extreme that the structure crashed into the water.

WORDS to KNOW

vortex: a whirling mass of air.

aerodynamic: dealing with the motion of air.

Engineers at the time didn't know much about **aerodynamic** forces and how vertical winds would impact a suspension bridge. Once again, it was a disaster that revolutionized suspension bridge design. Because of the Tacoma Narrows Bridge disaster, engineers today conduct wind tunnel tests to determine how well bridges will endure high winds.

Take the Penny Bridge Challenge!

SUPPLIES: *ruler, 4 hardcover books, printer paper, 5 paper clips, 100 pennies*

Design and build a bridge that supports 100 pennies. The challenge? Use only a single sheet of paper and 5 paper clips.

1 Arrange the books in two stacks of two books. Position them 6 inches apart (15 centimeters). Use a single sheet of paper to span the distance between them. How can you fold, bend, rip, roll, coil, or twist the paper to make it stronger? How can you arrange 5 paper clips for stability and added strength?

2 Place the pennies, one by one, on the beam until structural failure collapses it under the load. Tally the number of pennies you used.

3 Back to the drawing board! Can you boost the number of pennies your beam will support? Use trial-and-error to figure out how to redesign a stronger bridge with the same materials. Test your new design and compare results with your earlier attempt.

TRY THIS

Galloping Gertie became famous as "the most dramatic failure in bridge engineering history." Research online to watch 1940 footage captured live at the time of Galloping Gertie's dramatic collapse. It's quite a shock!

Experiment With Corrosion

SUPPLIES: *6 sticky notes, permanent marker, 3 clear plastic cups, wax paper, ruler, water, table salt, spoon, white vinegar, 3 iron nails, timer, journal, pen, tweezers*

In 1983, the Mianus River Bridge in Greenwich, Connecticut, collapsed after 25 years of use. Engineers blamed corrosion and a crack in a pin supporting the structure. Corrosion occurs when metal is destroyed by a chemical reaction. Rust is a reddish-brown coating that forms on iron or steel when it is exposed to moisture and air. Corrosion takes place during this chemical reaction. Experiment with iron nails to observe the effects of corrosion. HINT: Use iron nails to get the best results.

1 Create six labels with sticky notes. Write two labels for each category: Water, Salt Water, and Vinegar. Attach one label to each cup. Then draw vertical lines down a sheet of wax paper so you have three columns. Place the remaining labels at the tops of the columns.

2 Use the ruler to find the point halfway up each cup. Mark each point. Fill the cup labeled "Water" with water to the halfway mark.

3 Fill the cup labeled "Salt Water" with salt to the halfway mark. Pour water into it. Make sure it doesn't overflow. Stir with the spoon until the salt dissolves.

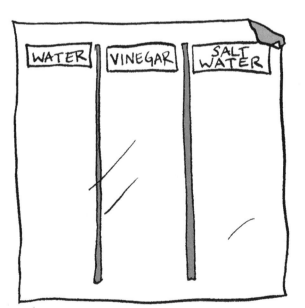

4 Fill the cup labeled "Vinegar" with vinegar to the halfway mark.

5 Place one nail inside each cup and set the timer for an hour.

6 In your journal, write down what you think will happen to each nail. Which do you think will show the greatest effects of corrosion? Why?

7 When the timer goes off, use tweezers to remove each nail from its cup. Place each in the appropriate column of the wax paper. Set the timer for 30 minutes.

8 When the timer goes off, study each nail. What do you observe? What changes have taken place? How accurate were your predictions?

• DID YOU KNOW?

The New York Thruway Authority handles about six yearly requests from motorists with gephyrophobia—that's a fear of crossing bridges—who need someone to drive their cars across the Tappan Zee Bridge. The motorists ride as passengers, and cover their eyes if they need to.

The Tappan Zee Bridge rises 150 feet over the Hudson River (46 meters). Its total span is 16,013 feet (4,880 meters). That's about 3 miles (nearly 5 kilometers)!

Liquefaction Action

SUPPLIES: *sturdy plastic tub, dry sand, brick, rubber mallet, bucket of water*

In 1989, an earthquake in Oakland, California, caused a 7-inch shift in the span of the Bay Bridge (18 centimeters). A 50-foot section of the bridge collapsed (15 meters). Liquefaction is a physical process that occurs during earthquakes, when sand turns into a liquid. It frequently causes ground failure. Simulate what occurs when an earthquake rocks a structure built over sand or silt.

1   Fill the tub about 2 inches from the top with sand (5 centimeters). Use your hands to spread the sand until the surface is smooth. Flatten any bumps to create a flat surface.

2   The brick represents a structure. Hold it vertically and push it into the center of the sand. Press on top of the brick to make certain it's firmly standing in sand.

3   Simulate an earthquake with the mallet by lightly tapping the sides of the tub. What happens to the sand? To the brick?

4   Slowly pour water into the tub. Continue pouring until water shows just above the surface of the sand. Wait 5 minutes to allow the sand to absorb water. In the meantime, predict what will happen when you repeat the simulation.

5   Simulate an earthquake again. Lightly tap the sides of the tub with the mallet. Now what happens to the sand? To the brick? What conclusions can you draw about what happens to structures built over liquefied soil?

Measure Motion With a Seismograph

SUPPLIES: *metal or plastic clothes hanger, piece of cardboard, masking tape, countertop, several heavy books, low table, string, scissors, marker, sheet of printer paper, block of wood, hammer*

Seismology is the study of earthquakes. Geologists are scientists who study the structure of the earth and monitor earthquakes. Make your own seismograph to measure motion.

1 Use the hanger, cardboard, and tape to create a mounting. Tape the hanger's wide ends onto the cardboard. Then, position the cardboard so it lies flat on top of a counter with the hanger's hooked end extending over the edge. Place books on the cardboard to keep it in place.

2 Move the low table beneath the hook of the hanger. Tie one end of the string to the hook. Determine the length of string you'll need to reach from the hanger to the top of the table with the marker tied to the other end. Cut off the necessary length.

3 Place the sheet of paper on the table. Make sure the marker tip touches it. If it doesn't, make adjustments.

4 With one hand, hold the block of wood against the side of the table. With the other hand, carefully tap the block with the hammer. The marker should draw on the paper to illustrate the push and pull of waves. What difference do you notice between push waves and pull waves?

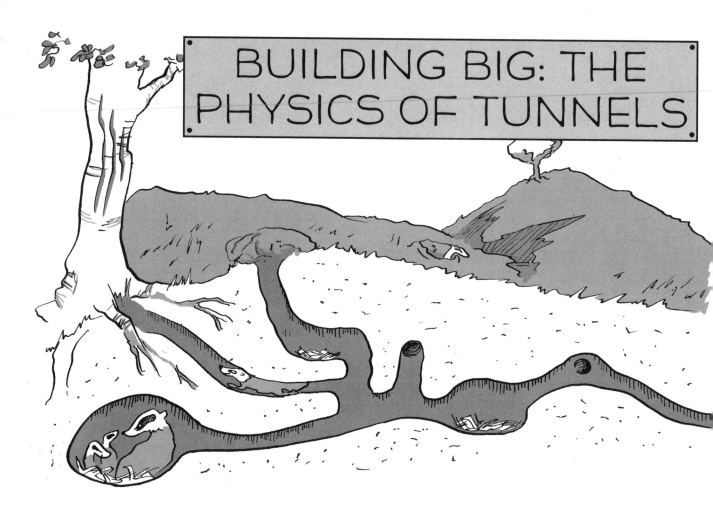

BUILDING BIG: THE PHYSICS OF TUNNELS

TUNNELS ARE PASSAGEWAYS THAT ARE ENCLOSED underground or underwater. Built with openings at opposite ends, tunnels are hollowed out of rock and soil. Like bridges, some tunnels occur in nature.

NATURAL TUNNELS

Animals are the engineers for many tunnels. Chipmunks and moles, for example, build snow tunnels to safely scurry to winter food stashes. Badgers' strong claws dig elaborate mazes of tunnels and chambers called "sets." Prairie dogs burrow underground to excavate "towns."

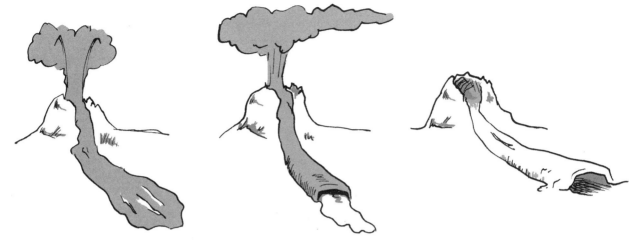

Rock formations create other tunnels. Maybe you've explored a **cave**. **Lava tubes**, like the Thurston Lava Tube in Hawaii and the Lava River Cave in Flagstaff, Arizona, are natural tunnels. After a volcano erupts, molten rock flows from a **vent**. When the top and bottom areas of lava cool, the lava in the middle can continue to move. After it cools, it can leave a hollowed-out formation like a tunnel or cave.

WORDS to KNOW

cave: a natural underground opening connected to the surface, large enough for a person to enter.

lava tube: a natural cave or tunnel that forms when lava flows from a volcano.

vent: an opening in the earth's crust that releases gas and molten rock.

DID YOU KNOW?

Cooled lava forms special kinds of stalactites. These are formations that hang from the ceiling of a cave. They're called lavacicles because they look like icicles! Caves are often connected by networks of tunnels. They can form from water eroding rock over long periods of time.

MANMADE TUNNELS

Manmade tunnels are one of the earliest structures built by humans. Historians believe ancient people dug them to make larger living spaces in caves.

Like bridges, tunnels advanced civilization. Early civilizations built some tunnels to **irrigate crops**. They constructed others to deliver fresh water supplies and flush away **sewage**. By the time of the Industrial Revolution, engineers were blasting through mountains. As time progressed, engineers found ways to dig beneath rivers and lakes. They built undersea tunnels that withstood weight from crushing waters.

Today's engineers construct some tunnels under highways and railways to ease traffic congestion. Other tunnels are critical to **infrastructure**. These underground systems supply a community's water, power, and communications networks. Tunnels protect data, electrical, and cable television lines.

PHYSICS OF TUNNELS

Though bridges and tunnels are extremely different structures, their engineers use similar knowledge. To build structurally sound tunnels that don't collapse, engineers depend on knowledge of **statics**. Do you remember Newton's Third Law of Motion? "For every action (force), there is an equal and opposite reaction (force)." Tunnels rely on a balance of forces. The pulling of tension sends force from a tunnel to the ground all around it. The pushing of compression sends force from the ground all around the tunnel.

WORDS to KNOW

statics: the area of physics that deals with how forces work together to keep objects completely still.

Like a bridge, a tunnel must be strong enough to support the force of its dead load. That's its own weight. It must support the variable weight of its live load. That's the changing number of vehicles, passengers, and cargo that travel through it.

Tunnels are usually shaped like an arch.

The arch shape spreads the tunnel's weight so that it doesn't all sit above the arch itself. Some of the weight moves to the tunnel's sides and the ground beneath it. At the same time, weight from solid rock around the arch pushes. It holds the arch in place and prevents collapse.

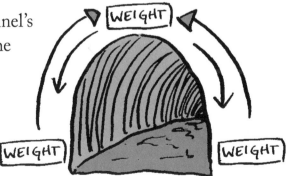

THREE STAGES IN TUNNEL BUILDING

Tunnel engineers dig into soft ground, through rock, and beneath water. Each set of vastly different conditions presents its own challenges. Yet, building in each requires completing the same three stages.

- **STAGE 1: EXCAVATION** In the first stage, engineers burrow through soil and rock. They hollow out a horizontal passage called a **bore**. Today, workers use a tunnel-boring machine to carve out the earth.

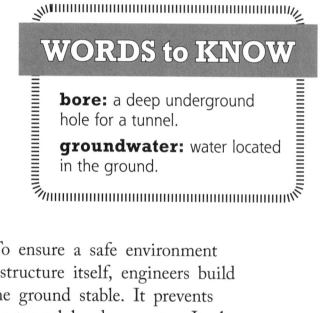

WORDS to KNOW

bore: a deep underground hole for a tunnel.

groundwater: water located in the ground.

- **STAGE 2: SUPPORT** Once tunnelers excavate a passage, there's a danger of collapse. To ensure a safe environment both for digging and for the structure itself, engineers build a support. A support keeps the ground stable. It prevents earth from shifting around the tunnel head, or entry. It also keeps **groundwater** from flowing inside.

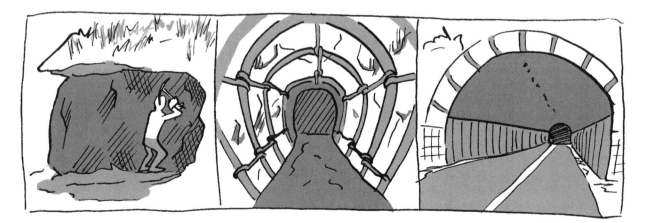

○ **STAGE 3: LINING** Even rock isn't always solid. Fissures are long, narrow cracks in the rock. They are hazards in construction because weak rock crumples. It splits into pieces when workers bore into it. To prevent collapse and hold slipping rock and soil in position, engineers build a lining inside the tunnel. Most modern linings are built with steel and are fireproof.

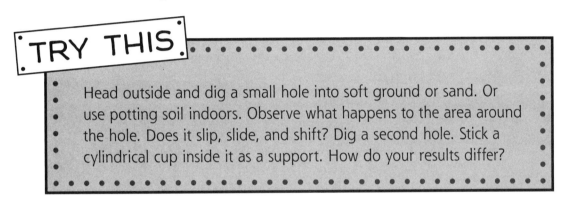

TRY THIS

Head outside and dig a small hole into soft ground or sand. Or use potting soil indoors. Observe what happens to the area around the hole. Does it slip, slide, and shift? Dig a second hole. Stick a cylindrical cup inside it as a support. How do your results differ?

TUNNEL TYPES

When planning tunnels, engineers have to consider all the challenges of a site, and study its environment. They look at a location's characteristics such as whether a body of water, a mountain, or another transportation route needs to be spanned. They collect and examine soil and rock samples. They determine whether there are any fault zones on the site, and they figure out the flow and pressure of the groundwater.

After careful consideration, engineers determine the best methods of construction and choose among three tunnel types. Each requires different methods of building big.

○ **SOFT-GROUND TUNNEL:** Soft-ground tunnels are critical to infrastructure. They house sewers. They move water supplies. When you ride a subway train, you're racing through a soft-ground tunnel. Workers hollow soft-ground tunnels from shifting gravel, sand, and silt. Squishy, waterlogged dirt makes these dug-out areas unstable. Because goopy ground doesn't stand up on its own, collapse is a hazard. To stop cave-ins, engineers build **tunnel shields**. Shields are temporary supports, typically made of steel. They support the tunnel head during excavation.

WORDS to KNOW

tunnel shield: a structure used to keep a tunnel from caving in during excavation.

○ **HARD-ROCK TUNNEL:** Have you ridden a train or car through a mountain? Most hard-rock tunnels are used as mountain railway and highway passages. To excavate hard rock, workers set off explosives to blast their way through it. They suck out deadly fumes with vacuums and haul out rubble. Hard-rock tunnels naturally remain standing. Unlike soft-ground tunnels, they don't need much support during excavation. Have you ever driven from San Francisco across the Golden Gate Bridge and through the hard-rock tunnel on the other end? It welcomes you with a painted rainbow around its entrance!

○ **UNDERWATER TUNNEL:** In Europe, the amazing underwater Channel Tunnel links England to France. In the United States, the Holland Tunnel runs under the Hudson River to connect New York and New Jersey. Constructing underwater tunnels beneath bays, channels, and rivers is especially tricky. The crushing waters of a big dig's site could pop the tunnel like a water balloon.

To hold water back, engineers of the past relied on pressurized chambers. But those were hazardous to workers, who suffered the bends. Today, engineers build modern underwater tunnels from prefabricated pieces.

Water is 800 times heavier than air!

TUNNEL SHIELDS

Starting in the 1880s, tunnel shields used compressed air. Compressed air supported tunnels and prevented flooding. Yet, toiling for long hours in compressed air meant workers faced decompression sickness. They suffered the same agonizing symptoms as the sandhogs who built the Brooklyn Bridge. Decompression sickness is called the bends because the symptoms cause victims to double over, or bend, in agony.

WORDS to KNOW

nitroglycerin: a flammable, explosive liquid.

flammable: easily set on fire.

RISKY CONSTRUCTION

Today, we consider tunnel building safe. In the past, this wasn't true at all. Big digs are complex. Over the ages, engineers have used trial-and-error to devise new methods of carving out tunnels. First, laborers used pickaxes to hack away earth and hand drills to bore holes. They painstakingly chiseled through rock. Hand excavation was backbreaking. Laborers squatted through broiling temperatures in tight spaces with their feet folded against dusty rock and their limbs stiff. With no air circulating, workers choked in swirling dust and ashy smoke. They gagged from toxic fumes. Construction plodded along by just a few inches a day.

In time, drilling by machine allowed workers to smash rock quickly. With a boom, explosives propelled construction, too. But black powder, **nitroglycerin**, and dynamite presented grave danger. Nitroglycerin, for example, could explode without warning. Nervous workers never knew when the **flammable** liquid might blast them off their feet to their doom.

RISKS

BACKBREAKING WORK

PICK AXES MAKE SMALL PROGRESS

TEMPERATURES SOARED

Cough

DUST CHOKED LUNGS

CRAMPED SPACES LEAD TO STIFF LIMBS

EXPLOSIVES OFTEN SPONTANEOUSLY COMBUST

London's brick Thames Tunnel, begun in 1825 and completed in 1843, is a marvel of engineering. At 1,300 feet in length (396 meters), it lies at a depth of 79 feet beneath the Thames River (24 meters). The tunnel was initially built for carriage traffic. But horse-drawn carriages never actually used the tunnel. Instead, pedestrians packed its underground shops and cafes. In 1869, the railway took over. Today, the Thames Tunnel is essential to "The Tube," London's iconic underground transit system.

At the time construction began, the drills and explosives that engineers relied on proved almost useless. How would they excavate mucky ground beneath the river? A French engineer named Marc Brunel (1789–1849) revolutionized tunnel-building with his invention, the tunnel shield. Brunel designed a towering box with 12 columns, each three "cells" high and protected by heavy plates. His invention allowed miners to access only small sections of waterlogged earth at a time. They quickly excavated each area, with the shield supporting them.

**The shield provided support in front of and
around the ground until workers built a lining.**

WORDS to KNOW

hydraulic: a mechanical device that uses pressure from a fluid to move.

methane: a colorless, odorless, flammable gas.

DID YOU KNOW?

The saying, "there's light at the end of the tunnel" means there's hope after a bleak time or difficult experience.

Work under the Thames moved at a snail's pace. One miner was placed in each of the box's 36 cells. Between the miner and the earth was a wall of wooden boards. The miners would slip out one board, excavate the few inches of oozy muck that was exposed, quickly push the board back in place, and then slide out the next board until each had carved out the area of his cell's wall. **Hydraulic** jacks then moved the shield forward, inch by inch. Digging advanced only 8 to 12 feet a week (about 3½ meters). Once miners excavated a section, bricklayers constructed a lining.

Though Brunel's shield was "groundbreaking," it had its problems. Water broke boards and flooded the tunnel over and over. Six men died during the construction of the Thames Tunnel. Brunel's son, also an engineer, barely escaped drowning when the tunnel's roof collapsed under water pressure. Engineers were able to drain the tunnel. Yet, the water itself was hazardous. Filthy with raw sewage, it gave off **methane** gas. When miners' oil lamps ignited gas, tremendous explosions rocked the tunnel.

After years of struggle, engineers finally constructed the lighted roadways and a circular stairway, and the Thames Tunnel opened. Millions strode its "shining avenue of light," including Queen Victoria. She knighted Brunel for his invention, which had made the milestone possible.

The Bends in a Can

SUPPLIES: *2 cans of the same carbonated beverage, 2 clear plastic glasses, pencil and paper*

Gas is under pressure in a carbonated drink. You can't see it since it's absorbed in the liquid. Until you pop the top! That's when the carbon dioxide gas releases and starts to fizz. Decompression sickness occurs when another gas, nitrogen, releases into the bloodstream and forms bubbles. Use a fizzy carbonated drink to simulate the bends. HINT: This simulation is messy! Try it in a sink.

1 Without shaking them, place both cans on a stable table or counter. Allow them to sit for 10 minutes.

2 Very slowly the tap on the first can. Count "one, one thousand, two, one thousand." About halfway across, stop briefly. Then open the tab the rest of the way, counting again so you open it slowly. Try not to move the can. Allow pressure inside the bottle to release bit by bit. Slowly pour the drink into one glass.

3 Observe the drink. Does it contain bubbles? Does it froth and fizz? What sounds do you hear? Draw a sketch of the filled glass and what you observe.

4 Open the second can in one swift motion. Pour the drink rapidly into the second glass. Does it bubble and fizz? Does liquid spurt over the top of the glass? What sounds do you hear?

5 Draw a sketch of the second glass. Compare and contrast the results. What conclusions do you draw about the bends? Why do you think it's important to move from pressurized chambers slowly?

Newton's Rocketmobile

SUPPLIES: *ruler, drawing compass, marker, 2 washed Styrofoam fruit or vegetable trays, scissors, emery board, 4 straight pins, flexible tip straw, clear tape, balloon*

Use Newton's Third Law of Motion to rev up a Rocketmobile. It uses pushes and pulls—or action-reaction force—to self-propel!

1 Make the base and wheels of the Rocketmobile first. Use the ruler, drawing compass, and marker to draw the shapes on Styrofoam trays. Draw one 3-inch-by-7-inch rectangle for the base (7½ by 18 centimeters). Draw four circles 3 inches in diameter for wheels (7½ centimeters). Carefully cut out the pieces. Use the emery board to sand the wheel edges and smooth out bumps to get them as round and as smooth as you can.

2 Assemble the Rocketmobile. Hold the Styrofoam rectangle flat. Using the straight pins to make axles for the wheels, stick a pin into the center of each circle and attach them to the sides of the base where the front and back wheels should go. The pins should be loose enough to allow the wheels to spin easily. Use trial-and-error to test the wheels until you find the proper fit for each pin.

3 Now make the motor. Bend the flexible tip of the straw upwards. Tape the straw along the top of the Rocketmobile's base, with the bent tip in the back and the hole facing up. The other end of the straw should hang over the other end of the base.

4 Stretch the balloon a few times to loosen it—but don't let it snap! Blow it up several times, and then let the air out. Carefully place the open end of the balloon over the bent tip of the straw. Tape the balloon securely in place. The balloon should remain in place when you blow into the other end of the straw to inflate it. Test the balloon to make sure it inflates.

5 Now you're ready to watch action-reaction in motion! Place the Rocketmobile on a smooth, sturdy surface. Blow into the straw to inflate the balloon. Tightly pinch the straw shut to keep the balloon inflated. Then release the pinched end. Watch the Rocketmobile move. How does it work? The balloon pushes on the air. Air pushes back on the balloon. The balloon pulls the Rocketmobile.

Notable Quotable

"Anything's possible if you've got enough nerve."
—*J.K. Rowling, creator of the Harry Potter series*

Water Pressure and Depth

SUPPLIES: *scissors, half-gallon cardboard milk carton, permanent marker, ruler, nail, masking tape, gallon of water, paper and pencil*

Pressure is a force against a surface. Hydrostatic pressure is a force exerted by a liquid. It occurs because of the force of gravity. Hydrostatic pressure increases as depth increases. Experiment with water pressure and depth. Ask an adult to supervise when you use the nail. HINT: This is messy! Conduct the experiment over a sink or tub.

1 Cut off the top of the milk carton. Use the marker to make a horizontal line close to the top on the inside of one side of the carton.

2 Place the ruler against the outside of the carton, on the same side with the inside mark. Use the marker to mark the carton at ½, 1, 2, and 4 inches down from the top (1, 2½, 5, and 10 centimeters.)

3 With an adult's supervision, carefully punch the nail through each mark. Try to make the nail holes the same size and be careful that the nail doesn't tear the holes.

4 Cut off a long section of tape. Tape securely over all the holes. Stand the carton at the edge of the sink or tub, with the taped area aimed over the edge, into the sink or tub.

5 Pour water into the carton until you reach the horizontal line you marked. Predict what will happen when you remove the tape.

When you swim at the bottom of a pool from the shallow end to the deep end, you feel more force against your eardrums as you get deeper. That's water pressure.

6   Quickly rip off the tape. Use the ruler to measure how far the water is spouting from each hole. Jot down the distances you observe. Which streams squirt farther into the sink? What variations in distance do you notice from the top stream to the bottom one? What happens to the streams when all the water trickles out? What conclusions do you draw about water pressure and depth?

TRY THIS

Extend the experiment! Dry the outside of the carton well and tape the holes again. This time test each individually. Fill the carton with water. Tear off only the bottom tape. Observe and measure the water stream. Dry the carton, tape the bottom hole back up, and refill the carton. Repeat the process, progressing from bottom to top.

Milk Carton Turbine

SUPPLIES: *nail, empty and clean quart or half-gallon cardboard milk carton, fishing line, masking tape, deep sink or bathtub, pitcher of water*

Make your own turbine to experiment with Newton's Third Law of Motion. A turbine is a machine that uses water or steam to produce motion. Observe equal and opposite actions. Ask an adult to supervise when you use the nail! HINT: Try this activity outdoors! Tie the string to a sturdy tree branch.

1 With an adult's supervision, use the nail to carefully punch a hole into each of the four corners at the milk carton's bottom. Poke nails into the carton from the sides rather than underneath. Open up the carton at the top.

2 Find the carton's top center. Punch another hole directly in the center. Push a length of fishing line through the top hole. Tie the ends together in a tight knot so the carton will dangle from the line.

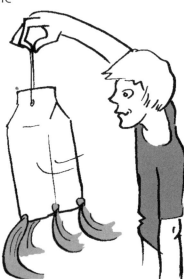

3 Use masking tape to completely cover all the holes. Pour water into the carton at the top. Hold it above the sink or tub, or hang it outside.

4 Predict what will happen as you gradually remove tape from the holes. Observe what occurs when you remove tape from one corner. What happens when you remove tape from two opposite corners? From all corners? You can dry off the corners and retape the holes to try different combinations. How accurate were your predictions? You should notice that as water gushes from the holes, the force pushes and spins the carton in the opposite direction.

AMAZING TUNNELS

FROM ANCIENT **AQUEDUCTS** ... TO HAUNTED TUNNELS ... to great escapes and wonders around the world. Tunnels are monuments to innovation and engineering.

WORDS to KNOW

aqueduct: a manmade channel that moves water by gravity, often in the form of a bridge supported by tall columns.

AQUEDUCTS

In ancient times, many civilizations built aqueducts, including the Aztecs, Assyrians, Egyptians, Greeks, and Romans. Primitive aqueducts acted as channels and canals. Many survive today.

Romans dug gently sloping aqueducts to transport water from sources of freshwater in the mountains to lower-lying cities far away. Gravity allowed the water to flow downhill. When Romans encountered a mountain blocking an aqueduct's path, they tunneled through. The work was treacherous. Squished in dark, confined spaces, workers heated rock with blazing fires. Then they cooled it with water so it split and cracked. Many workers who cut the rock by hand were crushed and killed by falling rock.

DID YOU KNOW?

During the Industrial Revolution, ships hauled goods and cargo from factories and mines. But as more goods were traded, these ships began to clog the waterways. To ease water traffic and open trade routes for freight such as coal and timber, engineers built canals with tunnels at either end.

EXTREME ENGINEERING

During World War II, prisoners of war engineered three secret tunnels from Stalag Luft III, a prison camp in Germany. It's a heroic story of innovation that sprang from a thirst for freedom. The imprisoned airmen used code names to identify the tunnels: Tom, Dick, and Harry. At Harry's entrance, they dug a trap door under a stove. Using materials scavenged from around the camp, they built crude hand tools and chipped away concrete and brick to carve a 30-foot entry shaft (9 meters).

The prisoners had to dodge guards who patrolled the camp with rifles and snarling attack dogs. As prisoners dug through the earth, they were somehow able to escape detection from microphones buried in the ground to hear digging sounds. Stashing dirt in bags inside their clothing, they sneaked tons of sand out from the tunnel. They scattered it around the camp gardens. They brilliantly used bed boards to line Harry with timber and pumped in fresh air through a string of empty milk tins.

After a year of secret digging, prisoners constructed an underground railway and an exit shaft. They packed the tunnel with smuggled food and water and stitched blankets into clothes for disguises. On the night of March 24, 1944, 76 prisoners fled through Harry. Within days, most were recaptured. But three prisoners who fled were able to escape to freedom.

RAILROAD TUNNELS

As the Industrial Revolution gained momentum, railways became more and more important. Steam-powered trains connected buyers with sellers. Factory owners in New England and the Midwest wanted to ship their goods to markets on the West Coast.

•DID YOU KNOW?

Gottard Base Tunnel, connecting Ertsfeld to Bodio under the Swiss Alps, is the world's longest railway tunnel. It was constructed with two parallel tunnels running 36 miles beneath the mountains (57 kilometers).

Farmers needed a way to move their products east and west. But there were many obstacles along the way.

In Massachusetts, Hoosac Mountain was a 5-mile-wide barrier blocking the way (6 kilometers). The state of Massachusetts knew it needed to build a railway to get through Hoosac Mountain. In the mid-1800s, Alvah Crocker, owner of Troy & Greenfield Railway, was determined to be the one to build it. Crocker set out to bore straight through the mountain. His plan involved building a horseshoe tunnel. Railway tracks would line the curved tunnel's flat bottom.

Crocker's builders planned a meet-in-the-middle excavation.

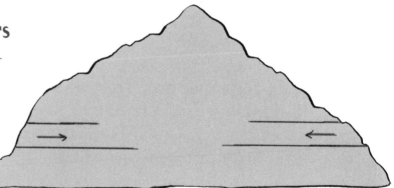

Laborers based at Hoosac's opposite ends would blast and drill a passage almost 5 miles long (8 kilometers). Eventually, they would meet in the center. The plan was risky because it meant that workers starting nearly five miles apart (8 kilometers), had to connect at a precise location. And if they didn't meet up, their grueling, hazardous labor would be wasted. Surveyors painstakingly took measurements.

They plotted a path like a treasure map to the middle.

Surveyors planned entries at the east and west ends. On the east, the rock was solid. But on the west, they found weak and crumbly soft rock. Miners called this kind of watery rock "porridge stone," and they feared the roof collapsing in on them. To protect themselves, they built girders that supported the top and sides of the tunnel.

PEACEFUL DYNAMITE

In 1866, the Swedish chemist, engineer, and innovator Alfred Nobel invented dynamite. The powerful explosive, made of sawdust and nitroglycerine, revolutionized rock blasting. Nobel, a peaceful person, developed dynamite specifically for construction. But his invention became a weapon of destruction in war. Nobel was heartbroken. He established the Nobel Peace Prize and, since 1901, the prize has honored people around the world for their work for peace, and for contributions in chemistry, physics, literature, and medicine.

STAR DRILLS AND GUNPOWDER

About 900 workers labored on the Hoosac Tunnel. Crews endured brutal conditions in the dim, broiling hot passage. Initially, they excavated by hand, walloping heavy **star drills** with 20-pound sledgehammers (9 kilograms). Men worked in pairs. One pounded a sledgehammer. The other swiveled the star drill after each whack to grind the rock. After pairs chiseled deep holes, they plugged them with gunpowder. Then crews covered their ears and scrambled in a mad dash to dodge deafening explosions. Squatting under timber ledges, they gagged on the dust and strained to see.

As was true of many of these early big digs, not everyone successfully bolted to safety. Some miners were hideously injured. Others died. In a week of earsplitting, dangerous labor, crews might advance only 15 feet (4½ meters). The project fell well behind schedule.

WORDS to KNOW

star drill: a tool with a star-shaped point. When struck with a hammer it can cut through rock and other hard material that would destroy electric drill bits.

NITROGLYCERINE AND PNEUMATIC DRILLING

Two innovations moved tunnel drilling and construction ahead by great strides during this time. Nitroglycerine, the powerful new liquid explosive, helped move the project along. When **detonated**, the flammable explosive demolished large chunks of rock. But nitroglycerine was very unstable. Sometimes it exploded without warning and caused sudden deaths. Pneumatic drills also changed the

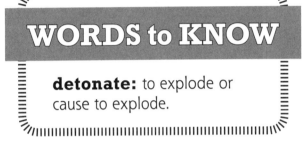

WORDS to KNOW

detonate: to explode or cause to explode.

way tunnels were built. They worked with compressed air generated by steam. These drills could bore into several areas of rock face at the same time.

Finally, in 1873, after 21 years of labor and 200 lives lost, workers met in the middle, completing the Hoosac Tunnel.

● DID YOU KNOW?

In the late 1880s, some people thought the Hoosac Tunnel was haunted. They heard sad cries coming from the tunnel at night and saw eerie blue lights flashing. People whispered that the ghosts of muckers who were crushed or killed in the project were hanging around the tunnel. Muckers were the workers who hauled away the shattered rock and other muck created by digging and explosions.

AMAZING TUNNELS 'ROUND THE WORLD

CHANNEL TUNNEL "CHUNNEL" (Connects England and France, 1994)

○ Railway tunnel that connects countries beneath the English Channel's wild, choppy waters, running 31 miles (50 kilometers), with 23 miles underwater (37 kilometers).

○ Links the island of England to continental Europe. Features two train passages and a service passage between them for fire escape and maintenance.

GUOLIANG TUNNEL (Tailhang Mountains, China, 1977)

○ Roadway tunnel that is 3,960 feet long (1,207 meters), 16 feet high (5 meters) and 13 feet wide (4 meters), providing one of the only ways to access a remote village in Hunan Province.

○ The tunnel is now considered one of the world's most dangerous roadways. Thirteen villagers engineered the tunnel, lined with rugged "window" openings, and they hand-chiseled it out of a mountain's rocky cliffs over five years!

HEZEKIAH'S TUNNEL (Jerusalem, Israel, 700 BCE)

○ Water tunnel that starts at Gideon Springs and runs 1,740 feet to Siloan Pool (530 meters).

○ Using radio-dating, scientists identified the ancient tunnel as one described in the Bible. King Hezekiah ordered construction to protect Jerusalem's water supply from attackers. An inscription at the site says tunnelers met in the middle!

LAERDAL-AURLAND TUNNEL (Norway, 2000)

° Roadway tunnel that connects Laerdal and Aurland, running over 15 miles through the snow-capped Sognefjel mountain range (24.5 kilometers).

° The world's longest road tunnel, its excellent air quality is achieved by large fans that suck out polluted air and bring in fresh air. To keep motorists from dozing off during the dull, 20-minute drive, golden light radiates from the floors. Like a bright sunrise!

SEIKAN TUNNEL (Japan, 1988)

° Railway tunnel that passes 33½ miles beneath Tsugaru Strait between the islands of Honshu and Hokkaido (54 kilometers).

° One of the world's longest rail tunnels, it's also the deepest. It's 787 feet below sea level (240 meters) and 460 feet below the seabed (140 meters).

TED WILLIAMS TUNNEL (Boston, Massachusetts, 1995)

° Roadway tunnel that runs 1.6 miles beneath Boston Harbor (2½ kilometers), connecting Interstate 93 with Logan Airport and relieving traffic congestion.

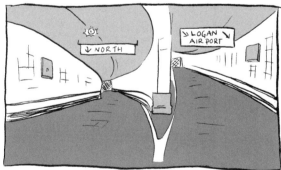

° Construction involved sinking prefabricated tube sections into place. Called the Big Dig, it was part of the United States' most expensive highway program. Price tag? $10 billion!

THE CHUNNEL

The Channel Tunnel, nicknamed the Chunnel, is one of the world's longest tunnels. Excavation began at opposite ends in England and France. Workers used a huge, snaking, tunnel-boring machine to hollow thick chalk rock on England's side. France's fragile, cracked rock proved more tricky. Engineers developed a special machine, part tunnel-boring machine and part submarine, to bore through it. Workers rode inside as they plunged beneath the sea. With 7,000 tons of water surrounding the machines, work was risky. The water pressure could burst through any leaks with a force that would crush workers and the machines. Workers used hoses and pumping equipment to battle seepage and fight disaster.

In 1990, after three years of laborious excavation, English and French workers busted through the last bit of rock. England's Graham Fagg and France's Phillipe Cozette met in the middle. In front of bright television lights and flashing cameras, a hole the size of a fist emerged from the rock. When it was large enough the two men reached out and clasped hands in a historic gesture of friendship and cooperation.

Waterslide Ride!

SUPPLIES: *2 clear milk or juice jugs, water, table, footstool lower than the table, about 4 feet of clear plastic or rubber tubing (1½ meters), 2 metal binder clips, paper clips, beads, or mini plastic toys*

A siphon is a tube that uses gravity and air pressure to transfer water by making it flow. With clear tubing and gravity, make a siphon that moves water from one level to another. Whisk little objects into motion! HINT: Is the submerged end of the tube floating to the surface? Use a rock to weight it down.

1 Fill one jug nearly to the top with water and place it on the table. Set the footstool on the floor next to the table. Place the empty jug on the footstool.

2 Fill the tubing with water from your sink. Use binder clips to clamp both ends securely shut. Place one end of the tubing into the filled jug. Place the other end into the empty jug.

3 Remove both binder clips. Observe what happens. Water should flow from the elevated jug to the one at floor level.

4 Modify the activity. Place the jugs in position in the same way, with the full one on the upper surface and the empty one on the bottom. Fill the tube with water and clamp the ends. This time, after unclipping the ends, slip paper clips, beads, or mini plastic toys into the end of the tube in the full jug. Watch them ride the waterslide!

ROCK TO WEIGH TUBING DOWN

Notable Quotable
"Be different. Think different."
—*Steve Jobs*

Steam-Powered Pinwheel

SUPPLIES: *scrapbook or origami paper 5 by 5 inches (12 ½ by 12 ½ centimeters), scissors, single-hole paper punch, push-pin, pencil with eraser, teakettle, water, stove, trivet, long oven mitt*

Create a pinwheel and use steam to observe the way steam turbines powered locomotives that once thundered through tunnels. HINT: You'll need adult help! Steam is extremely hot. It can cause burns, so use great caution.

1 Fold the paper on a diagonal from the top right corner to the bottom left corner to form a triangle. Make a crease and then open the paper. Fold on a diagonal again. This time, fold from the bottom right corner to the top left corner and make another crease.

2 Open the paper. You should see four triangles. Use scissors to cut along the four fold lines. Leave about ¼ inch uncut in each section in the center (½ centimeter). Don't cut all the way through the paper's center.

Notable Quotable

"You can't use up creativity. The more you use, the more you have."
—*Maya Angelou, poet, civil rights activist, and recipient of the Presidential Medal of Arts*

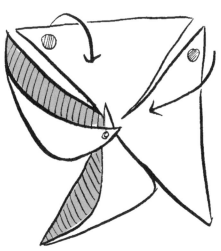

3 Starting in the lower right-hand corner of one section, punch a hole and continue moving the paper clockwise. Repeat until the lower right-hand corners are punched in each triangular section.

4 Fold each of the corners with a hole in it toward the paper's center. Skip corners without holes. You'll see a flat-fold-flat-fold pattern. You should have four folded and four flat sections.

5 Overlap the four folded sections at the center. Carefully press the push-pin through them and into the eraser end of the pencil.

6 Fill the teakettle with water. Ask an adult to place it on the stove to boil. Once the water boils, ask the adult to remove the kettle and place it on the trivet. Then, wear an oven mitt to hold the pinwheel above the steam coming from the spout. Make sure you keep your face away from the steam. What happens to the pinwheel?

Experiment With an Aquifer

SUPPLIES: *measuring cups, white sand, clear plastic cup, water, chunk of modeling clay, aquarium gravel (natural color if possible) or small pebbles, red food coloring*

An aquifer is a layer of rock and soil through which groundwater flows. Aquifers provided major underground water sources for massive Roman aqueducts. Water quality varied greatly from source to source. Experiment with an aquifer to discover how water supplies become polluted through layers of earth. The same thing happens today. People who drink well water need to be careful about using lawn care products or disposing of chemical household cleaners because they can end up in the drinking water.

1 Measure ¼ cup of white sand (30 grams). Pour it into the plastic cup. Use your fingers to spread the sand evenly around the bottom.

2 Pour water over the sand. Thoroughly wet the sand, but don't allow water to pool above it. Observe the sand as it absorbs water. Notice that some water collects around sand particles. This is the water that gets stored in the ground and flows from the aquifer.

3 Flatten the modeling clay between your palms. Place the clay "pancake" over half the sand and press it up against one side of the cup to make a seal on that side. Leave the other side uncovered, with sand showing.

4 Pour a small amount of water over the clay. Observe how water collects above the clay. Clay is a confining layer. The water will not pass through it and will only flow to the sand below not covered by clay.

5 Rinse and dry the gravel or pebbles to remove any dust. Use them to form another layer of earth. Cover both sand and clay so the entire surface is covered in gravel. Use your fingers to form a gravel slope. Start at a low level to make a valley and gradually increase the incline to make the slope. This represents the layers of the earth's surface.

6 Pour water into the cup. Fill the valley until the water reaches the top of the hill. What happens to the water around the gravel? The pores in the rocks and openings between them allow water to be stored there. This is called groundwater. Does the water form a little lake above the gravel? This is "surface" water. Both groundwater and surface water can be used for drinking.

7 To represent water contamination, add several drops of food coloring to the gravel hill. Try to keep the drops as close to the inside wall of the cup as possible. What happens to the food coloring? How much of the water source does it impact?

ACQUA PAOLA

In 1612, a Roman aqueduct was rebuilt that had originally been built by Emperor Trajan in 109 CE. The aqueduct was renamed Acqua Paola after Pope Paul V. Its water supply came from Bracciano Lake, a source that had become polluted and foul-tasting. Even today, Romans joke that if something is of poor quality, "It's a good as the Acqua Paola."

Meet You in the Middle?

SUPPLIES: rope, 2 chairs of the same height, large piece of cardboard, metal binder clips, 4 hardcover books, 2 round stickers, tape measure, paper and pencil, toothpicks

Workers built the Chunnel by boring through earth at opposite ends to meet in the center. Working with a friend, can you meet in the middle? HINT: Don't use light poster board or another product you can peek through!

1 String rope between the tops of two chairs and knot it securely in place. Find the center of the rope. Use binder clips to clamp the cardboard to the rope so the bottom touches the floor and it is centered. Place 2 books at the bottom of each side of the cardboard to steady it.

2 Sit on the floor in front of the cardboard, with your partner on the opposite side. Imagine the cardboard is a mountain you'll bore through. Choose a location to start the bore on your side. Mark the location with a sticker.

3 Use the tape measure to determine the sticker position. Jot down measurements.

4 Pass the tape measure to your partner. Explain the necessary measurements that reveal the sticker location.

5 Have your partner use the tape measure to try to find the same location on the opposite side and mark it with a sticker.

6 Carefully poke a toothpick through the center of the sticker on your side. Does it pop out in the center of your partner's sticker? How close to meeting up were you? What can you do to more precisely meet in the middle?

TUNNEL DISASTERS

PEDESTRIAN TUNNEL

SANDWICHED BETWEEN LAYERS OF ROCK DEEP IN THE BELLY of the earth, tunnels seem safe from disaster. But forces of nature, including **avalanches**, floods, earthquakes, and landslides can demolish them. Fires, structural flaws, and faulty building materials can also cause deadly catastrophes.

WORDS to KNOW

avalanche: a sudden and quick downhill flow of snow and ice from a mountain.

THE IMPOSSIBLE RAILROAD

No wonder it's called "The Impossible Railroad!" The San Diego and Arizona Eastern Railway was the United States' last **transcontinental** railway and the most expensive ever built. Through the treacherous and rugged Carrizo Gorge near San Diego, the track crosses 14 bridges and 21 tunnels in only 11 miles.

As soon as the railway opened in 1910, locomotives charged along this new gateway to the East.

WORDS to KNOW

transcontinental: spanning all or most of a continent.

During the railway's long life, its tunnels and railroad lines battled a string of disasters. In 1920, an avalanche blocked a tunnel. In 1932, a fire that blazed for four days collapsed one tunnel, and a landslide crushed a second tunnel. Another fire wiped out a third in the same year. In 1976, Hurricane Kathleen wiped out a railroad line in Carrizo Gorge.

CALIFORNIA

SAN DIEGO

PACIFIC OCEAN

MEXICO

14 BRIDGES
21 TUNNELS
ONLY 11 MILES LONG

THE "IMPOSSIBLE RAILROAD"

The railroad company came close to closing the route. But it kept the line open until 1984. After 20 years, the railway reopened in 2004.

FLOODING TRIGGERS DISASTER

In 2011, a private coal mine in Wales called Gleison Colliery flooded, collapsing a tunnel 300 feet beneath the ground (91 meters). Seven miners were trapped inside.

WORDS to KNOW

rabbit warren: a figure of speech used to describe connected underground burrows and tunnels where rabbits live.

seam: a layer of coal sandwiched in bedrock.

The mine had opened in 1993. Over the years, miners dug deeper and deeper into steep hillsides of the River Tawe. They drilled and blasted coal. Flooding plagued the mine and rain often filled mine shafts with water.

Journalist John Bingham of the United Kingdom's *The Telegraph* described the mine. "Decades of mining created a **rabbit warren** of tunnels and chambers . . . Two high-powered pumps are used almost constantly to keep the mine free of water, allowing a small team of miners to work the **seam** of coal." The seam was only 2 feet 6 inches wide (76 centimeters). Miners sprawled on their bellies to dig.

In September 2011, seven miners used explosives to widen the site. Water unexpectedly gushed into the mine, trapping them. Rescue workers tried to enter the tunnel the miners used, but water blocked their way. Divers plunged underwater to check out conditions. Debris jammed the murky waters and the divers couldn't see.

Firefighters tried to enter the air tunnel that led to the mine's surface. But there wasn't enough oxygen to breathe. Rescuers frantically pumped water out and oxygen in. Firefighters finally brought three surviving miners, one by one, to safety. Sadly, they recovered the bodies of the four other miners who had drowned in the disaster.

TOXIC CARGO

WORDS to KNOW

toxic: something that is poisonous or harmful.

derail: to accidentally go off the tracks.

thermal imaging: heat-sensitive devices that show images of people or objects.

Disaster will drive bustling cities to a screeching halt. It happened in Baltimore, Maryland, in 2001. Baltimore is a city of over 600,000 people. It's an important transportation hub for the CSX Railway. At about 4:14 p.m. on a hot July day, Baltimore's rush hour geared up. Baltimore Oriole baseball fans packed cars, trucks, and buses. They streamed toward the second game of a doubleheader in Camden Yards. Meanwhile, a CSX freight train was hauling **toxic** cargo through the city's Howard Street Tunnel.

Suddenly the train **derailed** and burst into flames inside the tunnel. The fire ignited what Michael Dresser of the Baltimore Sun called "a witches' brew of chemicals." If inhaled, the chemicals would burn people's lungs.

Toxic fires blazed through the tunnel for nearly a week. Temperatures reached a scorching 1,550 degrees Fahrenheit (843 degrees Celsius). Thick, black smoke poured from one end of the tunnel. At first, choking smoke prevented firefighters from even entering the tunnel. They used **thermal imaging** equipment to pinpoint the exact location of the blaze. Working in blistering heat and blinding smoke, firefighters stifled the flames containing toxic materials.

Amazingly no one was seriously injured or killed. But the fire impacted the city in many ways. The fire's heat caused a water main to burst and Baltimore's streets flooded. Roads into the city closed. Foot traffic disappeared. Internet lines were damaged. Businesses lost customers. For a week, downtown Baltimore was a ghost town. While the city recovered, chemicals left behind built up inside the tunnel. Months later, explosions blasted manhole covers into the air on Baltimore's streets!

THE FALLS ARE FAILING!

Poor engineering and overuse nearly brought down St. Anthony Falls and Hennepin Island along the Mississippi River in 1869. "The falls are failing!" A frantic cry rallied residents of Minneapolis and St. Anthony, Minnesota. People dashed to the falls to see the Hennepin Island tunnel collapsed and the Mississippi River rushing through a gaping hole. Hundreds of men tried to fill the huge hole in the rock wall of the falls. They cobbled together large timber rafts and weighted them down with soil and rocky debris to sink them into the hole. In time, they plugged it. Or so they thought.

Suddenly, rafts hiccupped. A whirlpool belched up gigantic logs. For an instant, rafts stood straight up like giant toothpicks. Then the fierce whirlpool sucked them down.

Why did the waterfalls nearly collapse?

During the 1700s and 1800s, visitors flocked to view the beauty of St. Anthony Falls. As more people settled the area, they built flour and lumber mills at the falls, which relied on waterpower. Mill owners built dams, canals, and tunnels to redirect water. This construction ate away at the stone beneath the falls. Over time the falls shrank and moved upstream.

In 1865, businessmen William Eastman and John Merriam bought Nicollet Island, just upstream from St. Anthony Falls. They planned to use it for industry. They began excavation of a 6-foot by 6-foot tunnel to run beneath Nicollet Island and its neighbor on the Mississippi, Hennepin Island (2 by 2 meters). The tunnel would bring waterpower to Nicollet Island. After they had dug through 2,000 feet of sandstone (610 meters), the mighty Mississippi River broke through the fragile stone and water gushed into the tunnel. A gigantic whirlpool spiraled and sucked everything in its path down the tunnel. The tunnel's roof caved in and parts of Hennepin Island and the falls were washed away. It took the U.S. Army Corp of Engineers six years to rebuild and restore the falls. The corps is still in charge of maintaining the site.

FREAKISH STRING OF AVALANCHES

In 2010, a blizzard hit Afghanistan's Kindu Kush Mountains along one of the world's most hazardous roads. At 11,000 feet, the road is also one of the highest (4,400 meters). The storm launched 30 deadly avalanches that swept cars and buses into a gorge. Snowy, rocky debris buried at least 2 miles of the Salang Tunnel (3½ kilometers), trapping motorists inside. Rescue workers and soldiers bulldozed tons of snow and rescued 2,500 motorists. But tragically, they also unearthed frozen bodies of people who had perished.

TRAPPED IN THE BELLY OF THE EARTH

It seemed like the whole world held its breath in 2010 when an earthquake rocked San Jose, Chile. A cave-in trapped 33 gold and copper miners underground, huddled in a cramped shelter they nicknamed Refuge 33.

Above ground, rescuers relied on engineering know-how. With a hydraulic drill, they bored through the mine's ceiling to create a communication link. Rescuers dropped food, water, oxygen, and medicine through the borehole. To keep miners' spirits up, they sent MP3 players loaded with music and passed along a projector and recorded soccer games. Frantic families and friends set up camp to keep watch. They named it Campamento Esperanza. Camp Hope.

Rescuers dug a rescue shaft with front-end loaders, hauling away 8 tons of rock every 12 hours. Finally, after 69 days, a rescue capsule eased down the shaft lined with steel tubing. Miners had lost weight during their ordeal, so one by one they fit inside the cramped cage to be hauled up to freedom.

A force of nature triggered the disaster. The dedication of people and the power of machinery triumphed over it. The whole world celebrated.

You're the Engineer!

SUPPLIES: *paper, pencil, aluminum foil, cans, cardboard, clamps, craft sticks, duct tape, emery board, file folders, glue, gravel, masking tape, milk cartons, paper clips, push pins, sand, scissors, string or twine, toilet paper or paper towel tubes, toothpicks*

Through innovation, engineers solve problems. Use the engineering design process to create a structure that solves a problem. Base the problem on one in your community, such as traffic congestion. Decide which will better solve the problem, a bridge or a tunnel. Think big! Then build small to make a prototype.

1 IDENTIFY THE PROBLEM What do you need to accomplish? Ask questions. Collect information. Decide on your goal.

2 BRAINSTORM POSSIBLE SOLUTIONS Let the ideas fly! Write down everything that comes to your mind. Afterwards, sort through your ideas. Zoom in on the idea with the greatest potential.

3 DESIGN AND DRAW A PLAN Draw a diagram and plan for your solution. Choose what tools and building materials you'll need.

4 BUILD THE PROTOTYPE Make a mock-up. Notice anything that seems like it won't work.

5 TEST THE PROTOTYPE Does it withstand forces and loads? Will it resist collapse?

6 EVALUATE SUCCESS What worked well or didn't work with the design? What adjustments will make your structure better? What other tools or materials can you use?

7 REDESIGN WITH IMPROVEMENTS Back to the drawing board!

Avalanche!

SUPPLIES: *tarp, large piece of cardboard, glue, aquarium gravel or small pebbles, cuttings from shrubs or plants, wax paper, measuring cups, granulated sugar, white flour, potato flakes, powdered sugar, table salt, corn meal, wheat flour*

Avalanches, caused by competing forces of gravity and friction, trigger deadly cave-ins like the one that crushed the Salang Tunnel in Afghanistan. Experiment with items that represent snow in a variety of consistencies and simulate a series of avalanches.

1 Spread out the tarp and place the cardboard on it. Glue the gravel or pebbles in several places to represent boulders on a mountainside. Glue shrub and plant cuttings to represent trees. Let everything dry.

2 Spread out the wax paper. Make small, individual piles of a cup each of the granulated sugar, white flour, potato flakes, powdered sugar, table salt, corn meal, and wheat flour (about 150–200 grams). Imagine each is a different snow consistency. Rub each between your fingers. Notice textures. Which is smoothest? Grittiest? Most powdery? Do they remind you of snow you've touched before?

3 Experiment with different snow layers to illustrate mountainside snowfalls. For example, pour a layer of granulated sugar over the cardboard. Add layers of white flour and potato flakes. Predict what will happen when you tilt the cardboard. How will different types of "snow" flow? What will happen to plants? Gravel?

4 Mix things up! Experiment with different consistencies and layering methods. Which combination creates conditions for a severe avalanche? Try adding ice chips to the "snow" layers. How do they impact the snow's downward slide?

abutment: a structure that supports a bridge, one at each end.

aerodynamic: dealing with the motion of air.

air lock: an airtight chamber between two areas of unequal pressure, in which air pressure can be controlled.

anchorage: a massive concrete slab driven into the earth to anchor, or ground, a suspension bridge.

aqueduct: a manmade channel that moves water by gravity, often in the form of a bridge supported by tall columns.

arch: a curved structure in the shape of an upside-down U.

architect: someone who designs large structures and provides advice on construction.

avalanche: a sudden and quick downhill flow of snow and ice from a mountain.

barge: a boat with a flat bottom used to carry loads.

BCE: put after a date, BCE stands for Before Common Era and counts down to zero. CE stands for Common Era and counts up from zero. The year this book is published is 2012 CE.

beam: a rigid horizontal structure that carries the load.

bedrock: the solid rock that lies beneath loose material, such as soil, sand, clay, or gravel.

bore: a deep underground hole for a tunnel.

bridge: a structure built to span natural or manmade obstacles such as rivers, bays, canyons, highways, and railways.

caisson: a watertight structure filled with air under pressure. It is used for underwater construction.

cast iron: a hard, brittle type of iron that lends itself to casting rather than pounding.

cave: a natural underground opening connected to the surface, large enough for a person to enter.

center of gravity: the point on any object where all the weight is centered.

chemistry: the science of how substances interact, combine, and change.

civilization: a community of people that is advanced in art, science, and government.

cofferdam: a temporary watertight structure pumped dry and used for underwater construction.

collapse: to cave in or fall down.

commuter: a person who regularly travels from one place to another to get to and from work.

compressed air: air that is under more pressure than the outside air.

compression: a pushing force that squeezes or presses a material inward.

corrode: to rust.

crop: a plant grown for food.

dead load: actual, constant weight of a structure.

deck: the roadway of a suspension bridge, which hangs from cables.

decompression: a drop in water pressure.

derail: to accidentally go off the tracks.

detonate: to explode or cause to explode.

energy: the ability to do work.

engineering: the work an engineer does, using science and math to design and construct structures.

engineer: someone who uses science and math to design and construct structures such as buildings, bridges, and tunnels.

evolve: to change or develop slowly, over time.

fault zone: an area that is at risk of earthquakes.

flammable: easily set on fire.

force: a push or pull that changes an object's motion.

geometry: the branch of math that looks at the relationship of points, lines, surfaces, and shapes.

girder: a large beam, often made of steel.

Gothic: a style of architecture that features pointed arches.

gravitational pull: the pull of objects to the surface of the earth.

gravity: a physical force that draws everything toward the center of the earth.

Great Depression: a time in United States history when the economy struggled and many people lost their money, homes, and jobs.

groundwater: water located in the ground.

Herculean: great strength or effort.

hydraulic: a mechanical device that uses pressure from a fluid to move.

Industrial Revolution: a period of time beginning in the late 1700s when people started using machines to make things in large factories.

infrastructure: public works that support a community, such as water and power supplies.

ingenuity: being clever, original, and inventive.

innovation: a new product or way of doing something.

interaction: how things work together.

irrigate: to move water from one area to another, usually for crops.

keystone: a wedge-shaped stone that locks the two sections of a Roman arch in place.

laborer: someone who does physical work using his or her hands.

lava tube: a natural cave or tunnel that forms when lava flows from a volcano.

legacy: something handed down that has long-lasting impact.

level: a tool made with a tube that holds liquid with an air bubble. It is used to measure a horizontal plane.

live load: the changing weight of vehicles and pedestrians placed on a structure.

load: an applied force or weight.

manmade: something made by humans, such as plastic and glass.

matter: a substance that takes up space.

methane: a colorless, odorless, flammable gas.

modification: a change.

molten: turned into liquid through heat.

mortar: a mixture of cement, sand, and water that dries hard like stone. It is like glue holding bricks or stones together.

natural resource: something from nature that people can use in some way, such as water, stone, and wood.

nitroglycerin: a flammable, explosive liquid.

open-ended: able to adapt to the needs of a situation.

physics: the science of how matter and energy work together. Matter is what an object is made of. Energy is the ability to perform work.

pile driver: a large machine that pushes posts into the ground.

pioneer: one of the first to use or apply a new area of knowledge.

plane: a flat or level surface.

precarious: in danger of falling or collapsing.

prefabricated: made in pieces or sections, then put together at a construction site.

prototype: a working model or mock-up that allows engineers to test their solution.

protractor: a semicircular instrument used to measure and construct angles.

pulley: a simple machine consisting of a wheel with a grooved rim that a rope or chain is pulled through to help lift up a load.

rabbit warren: a figure of speech used to describe connected underground burrows and tunnels where rabbits live.

raw material: something used to make something else. Natural resources are raw materials.

rivet: a short metal pin or bolt for holding together two plates of metal.

seam: a layer of coal sandwiched in bedrock.

seismic: caused by Earth's vibrations and tremors during an earthquake.

sewage: waste water, carried away through sewers.

shear: a sliding force that slips parts of a material in opposite directions.

solution: an answer to a problem.

sphere: round, like a ball.

star drill: a tool with a star-shaped point. When struck with a hammer it can cut through rock and other hard material that would destroy electric drill bits.

statics: the area of physics that deals with how forces work together to keep objects completely still.

stonemason: a person who is skilled in building with stone.

structural collapse: failure of a building, bridge, tower, or other structure.

structure: a bridge, tunnel, building, or other object built from a number of different parts that are put together in a certain way.

surveyor: someone who uses math to measure angles, distances, and elevations on the earth's surfaces.

suspension cable: a cable used to make a suspension bridge.

technology: scientific or mechanical tools and methods used to do something.

tension: a pulling force that pulls or stretches a material outward.

tetrahedron: a pyramid containing four triangular faces.

thermal imaging: heat-sensitive devices that show images of people or objects.

torsion: a twisting force that turns or twirls a material.

toxic: something that is poisonous or harmful.

transcontinental: spanning all or most of a continent.

trial-and-error: trying first one thing, then another and another, until something works.

truss: a rigid framework of beams or bars that supports structures such as bridges.

tunnel: a passageway that goes through or under natural or manmade obstacles such as rivers, mountains, roads, and buildings.

tunnel shield: a structure used to keep a tunnel from caving in during excavation.

vent: an opening in the earth's crust that releases gas and molten rock.

vortex: a whirling mass of air.

World Heritage Site: a place listed by the United Nations Educational, Scientific and Cultural Organization (UNESCO) as having special cultural or physical importance.

wrought iron: an iron that can be worked when it is hot. It is not brittle like cast iron.

BOOKS

Bell, Jacqueline. *Structures (Physical Science)*. Gareth Stevens, 2003.

Brimmer, Larry Dane. *Subway: The Story of Tunnel, Tubes, and Tracks*. Boyds Mills, 2004.

Brown, David J. *Bridges: Three Thousand Years of Defying Nature*. Firefly Books, 2005.

Harper, Suzanne. *The 10 Most Amazing Bridges*. Rubicon, 2007.

McCauley, David. *Building Big*. Houghton Mifflin, 2000.

Sullivan, George. *Built to Last: Building America's Amazing Bridges*, Dams, Tunnels, and Skyscrapers. Scholastic, 2005.

Pearson, Deborah. *Hidden Worlds: Amazing Tunnel Stories*. Annick Press, 2002.

Wolny, Phillip. *High-Risk Construction Work: Life Building Skyscrapers, Bridges, and Tunnels*. Rosen, 2009.

MEDIA

History Channel: *The Brooklyn Bridge*. A&E Television Networks, 1995.

History Channel: *Golden Gate Bridge*. A&E Television Networks, 2005, 1994.

Greatest Inventions With Bill Nye: *Engineering and Architecture*. Discovery Education, 2007.

WEB SITES

BBC documentary: Spanning the World: The Brooklyn Bridge: www.bbc.co.uk/worldservice/documentaries/2010/02/100209_spanning_the_world_pt1.shtml

Engineer Girl! www.engineergirl.org/

Discover Engineering: www.discoverengineering.org/

Discovery Channel: Extreme Engineering dsc.discovery.com/convergence/engineering/engineering.html

Newton: Ask a Scientist at Argonne National Laboratory www.newton.dep.anl.gov/askasci/engine98.htm

PBS: Building Big, www.pbs.org/wgbh/buildingbig/

San Francisco-Oakland Bay Bridge: baybridgeinfo.org/

San Francisco-Oakland Bay Bridge Construction Cams: baybridgeinfo.org/construction-cams

San Francisco-Oakland Bay Bridge, historical film: baybridgeinfo.org/history#.TpXjKJz9WuQ

Smithsonian Channel: How to Build a Tunnel: www.smithsonianchannel.com/site/sn/video/player/latest-videos/related/how-to-build-a-tunnel/390567893001/

Women at Work Museum: www.womenatworkmuseum.org/envision-engineering.html